On Being a Friend

Other Continuum books by Eugene Kennedy

Crisis Counseling

Sexual Counseling

On Becoming a Counselor

St. Patrick's Day with Mayor Daley
and Other Things Too Good to Miss

On Being A Friend

Eugene Kennedy

CONTINUUM • NEW YORK

1982

The Continuum Publishing Company
575 Lexington Avenue, New York, N.Y. 10022

Printed in the United States of America

Library of Congress Cataloging in Publication Data

Kennedy, Eugene C.
On being a friend.

1. Friendship.   I. Title.
BJ1533.F8K38   158'.25   82-1428
ISBN 0-8264-0186-4   AACR2

For my dearest friend,
Sara,
and for our great friends
Dick and Dorothy Trezevant

Contents

Introduction

ANY understanding of friendship depends on an appreciation of paradox. We can only draw close together, for example, because we are separate individuals. This is common sense and taken for granted. We learn, finally, that we do not stay close together unless we allow each other to remain, in some sense, separate. This is common sense too, but it is harder to learn. Friendship, which sings of union, inevitably confronts apartness, the strangeness and impenetrability of each of our persons. Assault that as if it were Everest and we never reach the top. As we learn to live actively with the mystery of closing the distance between us by respecting it, by letting it be, we discover friendship that grows stronger every day. Friendship does not work when people try to cement their relationship to each other by every legal and psychological fixative. Friendship thrives, like so many natural and human things, when we acknowledge its mystery and give it room in which to grow.

The central thesis of these reflections is built on the

most fundamental psychological paradox of our age: Friendship and death are closely related. We cannot understand and deal with one of these experiences without also dealing with the other. They may seem opposites—the one the fullness of life, the other the dark emptiness at its far edge—and yet, as with separation and closeness, friendship and death are aspects of the mystery that spreads across all our days. Its shadow falls on everything human.

Many of the struggles of contemporary men and women arise from their difficulty in perceiving the relationship between the many elements of life that they consider antagonistic and mutually exclusive. At least half the published self-help books provide cunning strategies to outwit the paradoxical nature of our existence. They proffer suggestions that often emphasize but one side of the tricky challenges involved in being human. They dilute death so that we can take at least half a look at it, a look that blurs the core dimension of loss. They offer emotional tricks to bind others into no-fault relationships in which the terrible danger of hurt has been eliminated or constrained. An entire generation, according to social commentators, struggles mightily under the burden of relationship difficulties because they cannot break out of their own narcissistic self-absorption. Having so distorted the emphasis on number one, they find that it is indeed lonely at the top. The paradox completes its cycle as their seeming victories over life turn sadly into defeat.

The contrasting mysteries of human relationships are inseparable strands of the same necklace of reality. Friendship does not enter our lives free of the imprint of death. The extraordinary experiences of life are finally found to reside not in the exotic but in the ordinary, the commonplace, the almost unnoticed transactions of every day. Mature people, out of step with trends, know that gratification can be delayed, sometimes for long periods, and that it can be greater and more meaningful because of it. There is a reciprocity between giving and receiving that reasserts itself in everyone's life. The ethic that liberation of the personality follows from acting out every impulse has proved to be hollow. We make no passage to friendship or enduring happiness that does not lead us through the shadowed valley of loss and death. The solutions that are proposed to avoid the paradoxical nature of our lives turn out to be problems themselves.

Friendship is not, then, an easy or sentimental trophy. Death is not a yawning void and the losses we face daily are not meaningless. We are processing these perennial mysteries all the time, touching and being touched by them. This book is a series of reflections designed to help us understand something of the truth about the experiences that are decisive in our being human. Breaking out of narcissism means breaking into the world of mystery in which love and death walk always hand in hand.

On Being a Friend

Elijah came to a cave, where he took shelter. Then the Lord said, "Go outside and stand on the mountain before the Lord; the Lord will be passing by." A strong and heavy wind was rending the mountains and crushing rocks before the Lord— but the Lord was not in the wind. After the wind there was an earthquake—but the Lord was not in the earthquake. After the earthquake there was fire—but the Lord was not in the fire. After the fire there was a tiny whispering sound. When he heard this, Elijah hid his face in his cloak and went and stood at the entrance of the cave.

1 Kings 19:9, 11–13

ONE

Which World Do We Live In?

SUCH simple questions are always difficult. We take our world for granted and move through it, in big towns and small, with as much ease and familiarity as the conditions allow. But the physical environment is merely one aspect of our world. Research, building on common sense, reveals that most of us have a rather narrow imaginative map of our own locality. It centers on the routes that we habitually take and, while these are swollen paths in our mind's eye, the rest of the territory falls vaguely away, as uncharted as it is usually unseen. The context of our familiar travels is not sharply defined. Otherwise natives in cities and towns could always offer exact directions, instead of the unspecified and sometimes qualified instructions they often do give.

The psychological environment, however, is our true habitat—the sprawling map, pulled now this way and now that by its competing designers, that we take as a rough approximation of reality. Do we question its construction or its influence on us? It is relatively easy

17

to observe others who seem to perceive things awkwardly. We are forever telling them that they are "living in a world of their own," and that they "should come back into the real world." We even feel self-satisfied when we give such practical advice. But what about our own world, the one we are sure is the "real" one?

Many influences weigh upon us as, through some integrative process within us, we stitch together our reasonable facsimile of the universe in which we live every day. There are many who are quite willing to tell us what the world is like and to guide our choices of direction in it. There are factors within ourselves—various needs, for example—which, whether we are aware of them or not, play an important role in building our functional picture of the world, that is, the one we use to interact with the world. Everyone has had the experience of "seeing" people when there is a powerful need to find them. In a crowded airport we see the persons we are looking for many times when we are particularly anxious about meeting them. People who in other circumstances would not resemble them at all suddenly, from the back or in a certain light, seem startlingly like them.

Perhaps the most significant sources of our ideas about our world, however, are the media—newspapers, magazines, television, and the movies. They understand their commercial power, but they show little consciousness of the manner in which, for literally millions of people, they draw the dimensions of the environment. They actually create the world for many individuals who live in and with this media-derived structure as though it were an accurate reflection of the real world.

There are subtle aspects to this because, in many

major events, people distrust the media. Still, we cannot totally escape the media's influence because the environment they describe is so pervasive and all-embracing. It takes a steady detachment to distinguish the environment created by the media like a great stage set around us from the truth of the world. What we term "news" is the classic example. The "news" is actually a special phenomenon, compounded of first fragmentary reports and rumors about certain events as well as the internal demand "news" itself generates for something novel if not downright shocking. The "news" is not necessarily related to fact, information, or truth, although it may be. It is an entity in its own right, and it feeds on the dramatic and the negative, on the old notion of the man who bites the dog. So headlines and lead stories tend to distort the world because they are reports on sensational and sometimes horrible events, on murders and wars, on scandal and graft, on everything, in other words, that is going wrong with the world. And this can be seasoned with whatever prejudices, to the Right or Left, dominate the editorial staff.

What is obvious, however, is that this sensational environment does not faithfully represent the real world. It projects a fraction of it, necessarily distorting it. That is the nature of the media business. It constantly supplies new worlds, none of them fully the real world. The problem is that, because the media are so powerful in their effects, many persons take their daily creation as the real world. Walter Cronkite used to end twenty some minutes of highly selective news reporting by saying, "And that's the way it is." But was it, really? It is very difficult to maintain enough balance to recognize that the evening news is only that and not the fullness of our world, or even of our city or town; these are far richer in reality than that which is transmitted by television, newspaper, or magazines.

If persons did nothing but watch television all day they would have a strange idea of the universe. It would be unsafe to go out at all, and between a surfeit of old movies and new movies attempting to look like old movies, a person's time sense could be badly distorted. If they watched game shows they would conceive of men and women as greedy and entirely foolish people, conditioned to beg for prizes the way lower animals can be conditioned to beg for food. And, to read the magazines aimed at the large market of young and not-quite-so-young adults, Americans would see themselves constantly puzzled about the central life mysteries of love, friendship, and death. These are not "new" entities, but the solutions proposed for dealing with them certainly are. Is this media-created environment about these essential life experiences truly trustworthy? Love, friendship, and death are inextricably interrelated. Their lines constantly cross and recross, occasionally looping far out from each other, but inevitably joining again. They are the mysteries of existence with which we must come to terms; they lie beneath the surface of every day. We cannot beat or outwit them. And yet the media make that seem possible.

Anyone who doubts the way in which this man-made environment can affect human conduct need only look around at those who strive to make themselves over in the latest fashionable image in some eager attempt to be up-to-date and, therefore, filled with contemporary grace. The pain that many persons find as their reward is bewildering. Here they have got the right running shoes and the latest speakers for their stereo, they are following the trends in sex, and, saddest of revelations, they are still not happy. They have followed the map and it has led to a barren land.

Love and death are subjects always being reworked by the media. The difficulty lies in the fact that we are suddenly surrounded by experts who are creating an environment of how to love and how to die, of how to survive grief, and of how to manage a hundred other aspects of these major mysteries of existence. It is a moment for caution because, if the Lord is not in the whirlwind or in the earthquake, neither is wisdom in popularized renderings of serious scientific or philosophic approaches to love, friendship, or death. What is pressed upon us as the great popular judgment on any subject, from friendship to death, is more often a reflection of the forces, many of them superficial, that feed the voraciously hungry media.

The fact is that nobody knows how to make friends or how we should die and there are no "how-to-do it" kits that can either educate or make us wiser about the losses and griefs of either experience. These are subjects too important to be left to the popularizers, to the entrepreneurs and designers of a cultural surround that has enormous breadth but not nearly enough depth.

Friendship looms large in the stage set of the popular media because there is so much confusion about it and longing to experience it. The last decade, however, with its obvious emphasis—hyped constantly by the media—on getting one's share ahead of everyone else in the great self-gratification derby, has crippled the capacity of many to enter into and to sustain truly reciprocal personal relationships. The shadows of death and loss fall across this pining for friendship, for it suggests that something human was lost in the great interpersonal revolution and that the loss has not been made up for yet. There is a mood of mourning for friendship, that once-great mainstay of life, which has been missing in the heady action of self-fulfillment. The paths of the abiding human mysteries cross in the contemporary search for ways of forming relationships that will survive the onslaughts and small deaths of life's long haul.

The gloss of the self-oriented seventies has dulled, and ordinary men and women want something more substantial than easy liaisons, a spurious sexual freedom, or lives lived out trimphantly alone. People want to be friends and they want to have friends.

Friendship and love are the only mysteries strong enough to stand up to and overcome their dark sister mystery of death. Much of the modern world's wailing and mourning rises off the blunted talent for friendship that is narcissism's inheritance. Many young people are literally stuck in a phase of self-absorption and do not know how to free themselves. They have lost something. Is there any wonder that they mourn? Their problem is complicated because the step in psychological growth that is missing can only be taken in and through give-and-take relationships with others, in and through enduring a death to themselves. These are what they have difficulty in establishing. The environment they grew up in has turned out to be an illusion. The scene has shifted, and they are so accustomed to placing their own needs first that they cannot comfortably respond in a situation in which they must do otherwise. They are handicapped in not having learned that life is only delivered when we know how to die.

The illusory environment created by the media is not the product of bad intentions. There is no conspiracy to deceive involved in the world spread out in news, advertisements, and soap operas. They are merely fulfilling their nature, which is to distract and persuade rather than to enlighten and make us wise. Persons who want lasting friendship will not look on this mockup of the world as their free environment. If there are no such things as totally happy endings with couples sailing off into a canvas sunset, neither are there easy and selfish passages into the heart of the experiences that are crucial to human development and a sense of meaning. We simply must walk past or through the environment of airy promissory notes about life and into life itself. We cannot muffle the drums of death; we cannot soften the potential loss that sharply edges every human relationship. In friendship and loss we look directly at the issues that are profound mysteries for those who love and frustrating puzzles for the self-centered.

When it comes to experiences that finally define us—love and work and living and dying—we must learn for ourselves. We cannot move with the herd in such areas, nor according to the plans, no matter how finely drawn, of those who pretend to know better than we ourselves about the main human chances in the only lives we have to live. We need to encourage each other to stand critically aside from the inundation of superficial material on friendship and the other great mysteries of life. These have been corrupted by those who approach these essentials of the good life as exploitable fads. We face and work through these experiences on our own to achieve the sense of our tragic grandeur that is essential to our wholeness. Nobody fakes that; nobody gets by on the outside of love or death.

TWO

The American Way with Mystery

MYSTERY, for many Americans, resembles a log fire in the living room. It is immensely attractive when under control, when its unpredictable spirit is penned, when, in other words, the inherent terror of fire is clearly tamed. It is not far different for the mysteries of life—of friendship and sex, of intimacy and mysticism, of suffering and death itself. We feel two ways about them: they attract us and put us off at the same time. We edge close to them, we revel or feel strangely excited and changed by them at times—and yet we do not wish to surrender ourselves totally to them. We want mystery, but we want it on our terms and under our control. We like our mysteries gutted of dread. They can be charming, titillating, or even comforting, but never, ever, terrifying.

To believe, to love, to be sexual—all of these are filled with mystery of the most compelling sort. And peoples' heads constantly teem with distractions or longings about one or all of these basic experiences.

The reason is simple: These are truly fundamental aspects of life through which we discover its meaning. In order to understand our existence we need to taste these mysteries—along with others such as hope, frustration, joy, separation, laughter, and death, yes, ever-present death, which is as sinew and bone to the structure of all these others.

We have, in fact, no choice about facing these overlapping experiences because they come with life itself. We do have some choice, however, about the way we face them. To look straight at them is to live with flames that may at any moment break out of the prison of the fireplace and engulf us. So, although we recognize their importance and sense their appeal, we still want control of them. We want the flame for the light and warmth, but we do not want singed hair or charred skin. Dangerous mysteries must be inspected carefully, from a distance or from the side.

As a result, many people flirt with mystery all the time but never really come in contact with it, never touch its core. They enjoy erotic enticement, but they do not experience sexuality. They check their biorhythms and their astrological charts for guidance, but they never really encounter the mystery of faith or belief. Fidelity, a further dimension of such mystery, must be profoundly terrifying because so many refuse even to take a look at it. Defensive, destructive wit has never illumined the world the way a rich and understanding sense of humor does. Pleasure, relatively easy to come by, never measures up to joy, which seldom comes without pain but which has a timeless quality to it. If infatuation breeds a thousand anxieties in return for its illusion, love and friendship deliver peace along with their bewildering daily challenge to sacrifice. Nothing is as bittersweet as separation, but as we cling to its raw edges, we touch a mystery that is as tender and powerful as the love of which it is always a part. How inadequate, how little to be weighed in the same balance is the diluted antidote of "togetherness"!

Love and death are the grand masters of mystery, and we do not like to look directly into their faces. We carry on with dimmed visions of both. We prefer to keep love and death slightly out of focus, or we strain to look away from or beyond their blinding light. We would tame them, as we do the fire, so that what is wild and unpredictable about them will pass under our sure control. If sexuality has been converted into sexiness, and friendship into mindless togetherness, death has been retouched, as if by a pale mortician's hand, so that we contemplate only its surface and comfort ourselves by saying how lifelike it looks.

Love and death are robust mysteries. They resist easy manipulation and they will not be tamed at all. Yet books, seminars, and academic courses continue the effort to master these mysteries of mysteries. Such efforts to guarantee success at friendship or to manage our way across the last threshold as though nothing had happened to us end up diminishing ourselves and our capacity to appreciate these commanding experiences of mystery. Educators have not been able to get sex education, or even arithmetic, right in the schools yet, so some hesitation about the value of courses concerning love and death is appropriate. Love and death are "in" for the trend watchers of benevolence who readjust their need to help in order to keep up with them; one season they are marching with the farm workers, the next they are dabbling in prison reform, and now, in hordes, they are "into" the new friendship and the new dying—other people's friendship and dying, that is.

What is the American way with such mysteries? First of all, we like to reorganize them, if at all possible, so that they possess a more logical framework, that is, so that they fit better into our understanding and respond more surely to our solutions for their difficulties. This American organizational approach represents a yearning, like that for old-fashioned movies with a beginning, a middle, and an end. It is optimistically embodied in the *Readers Digest* approach to things, which, on subjects as diverse as your child's I.Q., your sex life, or your blood pressure, describes, first of all, just how bad things are while it provides an escape ladder to health, success, and maybe even immortality at the same time. Organize the problem and *do* something about it; that's the American way. But can the great mysteries ever be organized; will friendship or death sit still for it? Mysteries are subtle presences in life and they disappear if the air is stirred by an efficiency expert who feels that he can measure them and perhaps even improve the angle of their sweep through life.

Just inspect our record with mystery. The more we have analyzed love, the more psychologists have broken it down into tricks and skills, the more elusive it has become. Only Americans could have produced the Human Potential Movement and its technology of workshops, study guides, and enthusiastic groupings, all bent on cornering mysteries of intimacy and growth. Where else could computer dating have been born except here? Has sexuality been measured or analyzed with greater intensity anywhere else in the world? Still, our wisdom about sex has hardly kept pace with the data unfurled like banners of a supposedly liberated age. The authentic mystery of sexuality has been grievously assaulted if not killed outright in the process. Even healthy eroticism has been stifled rather than freed through the vulgar acting out of the last few decades.

As Edmund Burke once wrote, nothing causes you to lose your audience more swiftly than telling them everything. Reports have now appeared in the popular press about the growing problem of asexuality, of a strange numbing of sexual desire and behavior in supposedly swinging metropolitan America. Perhaps it is only a sign of the way mystery dies in the midst of excess. The sin in the Garden of Eden may have been similar: a stupefying lust to seize the heart of mystery, to have the knowledge of the gods the easy way.

Now death, dubbed the "last taboo" until somebody started pushing incest into the spotlight, has been turned over to the managers of popular culture and commercialized wisdom. It has been grist for the mills of the organizers who, for example, have mistakenly made a rigid set of requirements out of Dr. Elisabeth Kübler-Ross's general observations concerning the stages of dying as experienced by the terminally ill. Courses have multiplied, books by the dozens have been published, cover stories have appeared in news magazines; death has clearly arrived. But much of the effort has been to make death, like friendship and everything else in America, equal. Death must be no different than any other experience; democracy makes every emotion available to the masses.

This American way with mystery reached a grotesque zenith in the report of the American Council on Life Insurance, which, according to news reports, predicts grotesquely that "as fear of the grave eases, car and home insurance may become more important than life insurance," and that "by the year 2000 old folks may be able to buy an 'adventure death' from a travel agency which will provide the purchaser with a romantic or historically inspired suicide." The report adds a note on what we may suppose will be the equivalent of food stamps in this brave new world. "For persons of lesser means," it suggests in tones as subdued as an undertaker's, "city governments provide service centers where one may die comfortably and be cremated at low cost." Here we have the organizers' triumph—a future environment in which death will be neatly and profitably incorporated into commerce and city planning. Death will have been overcome and nothing—not our deepest feelings for life or each other—will mean anything any more.

The problem with such preparation for the turn-of-the-century management of your death and mine is, of course, what it leaves out. Because these people do not understand love and friendship, they cannot understand death as a mystery intimately connected with these experiences. Death is not a disposal problem any more than love is a matching challenge for a computer. Friendship is not jolly acquaintances on a cruise ship and death is not one last great in-flight movie. It is also difficult to imagine any combination of functionaries intrinsically less attractive than those of the undertaker and the travel agent who stand grotesquely together in this surreal vision managing our meetings and separations for us.

Such a projected way of doing things is so hollow that it is already collapsing in on itself. These phenomena may be first-class symptoms of what Aleksandr Solzhenitsyn referred to in describing the shallowness of American spirituality in his famous 1978 graduation address at Harvard University. The vast majority of ordinary human beings possess spiritual sensitivity and a capacity to appreciate and respond to mystery. Solzhenitsyn may have missed the strength of this in American character, but so too have the educators and assorted do-gooders who are trying so desperately to homogenize the experiences of love and death. The mysteries of love and death are stronger than these efforts to bring them under control. And ordinary people know it. That is what the planners do not understand and have left out.

If we are overburdened with managers, we also lack desperately ministers or teachers who can speak to us in the authentic language of mystery. Those who should be most acquainted with mystery in our culture—especially the clergy—are all too often estranged from it. They may frequently be observed hurrying to catch up with the latest fad in the strange amalgam of psychology, positive thinking, glimmerings of oriental thought, and breathing exercises that is called spirituality today. Such individuals, caught up in their own needs, find it difficult to speak to human experience in simple and understandable terms. If you have never really been anywhere in your own life, that is, if you have never faced its pain or wonder on your own and have always let somebody else do your thinking for you, then you cannot help anyone else find their way in life. The basic problem for many supposed "spiritual" leaders is precisely that. They have sat in on the processes of friendship and of death for generations without sensing their profound relationship or understanding their meaning.

The response to Elisabeth Kübler-Ross's work has been enormous because she has stayed close to what people actually experience as they move under the shadow of death. She has learned something we already know. When people are dying simple things are important—their relationships with those they love and the experiences they shared with them. What we learn about dying deepens our understanding of living. It enables us to see quite clearly the experiences that are of lasting value. Friendship emerges as the bond through which the living share deeply the mystery of existence and prepare themselves for the challenge of death. Only love and friendship make sense out of life, only friendship and love are strong enough to vanquish the black knight of death. If mysticism is to be found anywhere in the universe it is wherever ordinary men and women touch the core of life by entering into the simple and abiding mysteries, such as falling in love, living their truth, or facing into death itself.

Friendship and death are intimately related. Their source is the same, their majesty is unparalleled, and their significance arises from their rootedness in what is human and natural for us. The only real preparation for the mystery of death lies in entering into the mystery of friendship. Neither mystery can be manipulated, however, and neither suffices for our human purposes in a watered-down state. It is through friendship and honest work that we touch the meaning of life. From them we draw the wisdom and strength to face the final mystery in the only manner that we can: together. Blessed are those unafraid to be friends, for they are also unafraid to die.

THREE

Death and Friendship

MUCH has been made of the *otherness* of death and of its alien and impenetrable nature. Death is pictured as concealing itself even as it supposedly reveals itself, so that we feel like outsiders in a matter in which, sooner or later, we will all be insiders. It is a mystery always turning the corner just beyond us; that can be our feeling as we view the unmoving dead.

When death is such a mystery, we approach it as we would a darkened house, vaguely uneasy as we strain to find a sliver of welcoming light. We comfort ourselves with metaphors of the familiar, through projections and interpretations that carry us across the barrier of death with images from our own experience. So we speak of death as relief and peace from the work and struggle of life, or as release and freedom from the constraints and imperfections of the human state. Death, we judge, takes us away from the limitations and the striving, the illnesses and the misunderstandings that ride point on the thousand plagues of our existence. The daily pain of being hurt, or being nice, or waiting for something better will vanish at death. Death will make us different; death will make us one with all being, egoless creatures of the Eastern way of looking at things; or it will make us perfect, achievers of the self-fulfillment that the Western world prizes so highly. We like to think of death as a cure for life.

But is this so? Is death a radically different state into which we can now journey, like science-fiction writers, only by way of our imaginations? If death really is a mystery, like every other mystery, it is already a part of our lives, scattering hints about itself throughout every day, touching and embracing us, now gently and now firmly, in the ordinary course of our human experience. Mysteries abound and one of their most salient characteristics is their familiar feel, that we have been here before, perhaps many times. Mysteries belong to ordinary life rather than to some distant realm of experience.

Mysteries are just on the other side of everyday experiences; they are the forces that pull the lines of our existence taut and open us, in our common rounds, to a timeless dimension of meaning. Mysteries are never totally alien to us; they are the deepest soundings of our lives, the great rhythmic movements of existence that are felt in everything human. But we do not see or understand any one of them completely at any one moment; we are too caught up in some individual aspect of love or dread or death to do that. Yet they signal to us constantly in the same way that the strung-out stars pull us toward their infinite distance; the same revelation rides the sea's vastness in the glistening waters of sunrise. The hint and the essential mystery are always connected, always part of the same experience; but frequently we catch only the surface signal—the bright stars or the shining water—and, catching these in our instamatics, we leave the larger mysteries to the special vision of the poets.

And yet they are present all the time, a partial revelation of the greater mysteries of which they are but a part. Death is, then, not some raging infection eating away at our experience, but an intimate and indispensable aspect of it. Death stands, holding a light for us, at the doorway of life itself. Death is everywhere, not only as the Grim Reaper in whose presence we shudder and repent, but as a constant mystery that permeates the universe of our physical and spiritual experience. Death signals us persistently about its own presence, not only in the physical decay and dissolution that are integral to the renewal of nature, but in the midst of the experiences by which we most proudly define ourselves as human, in every moment in which we truly believe, hope, or love, in every real experience of friendship.

Death is not just something *other;* it can never be understood that way. Death is, rather, a vital aspect of the familiar events through which we discover the meaning of our lives. Death is, therefore, linked intimately with everything that makes us fully alive. We grasp and let go of these riches every day. Our failure to see the link between friendship, that mystery of our affiliation, and death, that mystery of separation, makes it difficult to understand either one. These mysteries are the alternating tides of the same ocean, always overlapping, the one always a reflection of the other. Death is not a test coming in the unpredictable future. It is already here and we begin to understand it when we live with the dying, which, even in small ways, we find in every day of life.

Every day there are painful deaths charged with the demand for our realistic grief and mourning. These include the separations that accompany divorce or the natural growing up and growing away of family members. Every good family dies in order to give life to its members. Our daily deaths include the discouragement that the most ordinary men and women experience in simply trying to lead good lives. There can be a death that is hard to name in the restlessness and longing that invade even the most robust spirits at times. Count the deaths in loving or in striving for a goal; taste it in the tears of the brokenhearted. Drawing close to others in friendship necessarily implicates us in the potential for loss and hurt, for the deaths in a minor key that we suffer to make purchase of the riches of love. The more fully we are alive to spiritual realities, the more keenly we are caught up in mystery as the glistening edge of everything human.

Can we really associate friendship and death? Does not the thought of one exclude the other? Is it not too macabre to see a specter behind every embrace, to be troubled by separation even in our moments of deepest possession of each other? These are in fact the elements of dread that plague human beings, the intrusions about the ironic heart of existence that allow us to face and conquer it every day. Friendship without an awareness of death is bland and meaningless. Death that has no relationship to friendship has no power over us, no relevance to human existence. The mysteries of embracing and letting go, of friendship and death, are ever present. They constitute the one great signal about our transcendence.

Friendship is tested all the time by the small deaths, the almost unnoticed abrasions and wounds, so many of them unknowingly or unintentionally inflicted, that come so regularly in our contacts with each other. These are unmistakable signals about death's nature and steady presence with us. And we need to grieve and mourn these small deaths in order to find our way successfully back into life. That is the business of friendship—healing wounds, bringing us back to life, joining us together once more.

Consider an example of a small death in the midst of life. Find in it (for it is there) the whole mystery, leaf and flower, of our lives. Take an unreturned phone call from a loved one or a close friend. It is not a great matter, we say, but name, if you can, something that can affect us more deeply in everyday life. A phone call is the smallest of events and yet it is large enough, in its compact rendering of everything we prize, to hold the wonder and meaning of our lives. First of all, its very existence springs from a personal relationship of commitment and affection; it is at once symbol and expression of the friendship we value and count on to keep us alive. Yes, a phone call is a signal of that endless mystery that balloons out away from us like the galaxies.

Telephones are sometimes condemned as evidence of our materialism, as proof that we are tangled in our own polluting communications. And yet the telephone bears the weight of our hearts; indeed, its ring can stop our hearts, just as it can break them when, even on a small matter on a day among a thousand like it, it remains silent. So there is a special death for friends or lovers who have confidently waited for a call to be returned—surrendering a portion of their spirits in each passing moment that it does not come. We have all experienced the waiting that goes with such calls. It may be a call from a spouse on a journey, or from a child who has just returned to college, or from a friend whose support and counsel we need almost desperately. It can come from any direction and at any time.

We are uniquely vulnerable in such moments because our longing and trust—the whole movement of our hope and our love—may be found in miniature in the drama of the unreturned phone call. We may armor ourselves against the disappointment we feel, but denying its pain is a temporary help at best. We may say we do not care, or that it is just one of those things, but the truth is that we die as we speak these reassurances to ourselves. We die because we are disappointed in our expectation and, if it is a matter too small to mention or complain about, it is nonetheless a true reflection of how large our investment is in someone else. When we are intensely alive to other persons, we give them the power to hurt us, to kill the smallest portion of our spirit as an infarct kills a patch of tissue on the heart. Love involves us in the possibility of death all the time. Even these small deaths that we survive deliver a true tincture of the awesome mystery itself; we feel a sense of loss and consequent depression, an interval of grief and mourning, perhaps no longer than a moment, that is of the same nature as actual death and mourning.

Such deaths are as true as the friendship with which they are associated; they are neither the mock hysterics of the self-centered nor the imagined slights of the paranoid and the insecure. Love and death, on lesser and greater scales, are always intermingled; one is never found without some whisper or shadow of the other. We live a human drama that is almost a dance as we tentatively circle and then move closer to each other in the closeness in which we find life and death at the same time. There is no safe passage to intimacy, no enlarged life that does not demand death in some way from us. We cannot love or be loved without lowering our defenses against hurt, without inviting death into our lives. Deaths, small and great, become our constant companion when, paradoxically enough, we choose to live fully by assuming the risks of friendship and love.

Death is not a stranger to persons who understand that their fullest growth depends, not on grabbing everything for themselves, but on a readiness to give up much of themselves in loving self-sacrifice, in learning how to be friends. A willingness to die is always linked to the true discovery of life. The biblical writer Saint Paul spoke for everyone when he proclaimed, "I die daily." The difficulty for most of us is that we are too close to the mysteries in which we live to see them clearly. We do not understand, and, aside from the poets, there is hardly anyone who can explore the significance of the multiplied episodes of dying that accompany intense living. But death is sown deeply into our most important experiences, into those that give us title to the designation "human." There are small deaths in a hundred simple things, or in the awareness that time is passing, or that we are growing older, or that we cannot hold on to a beautiful but passing moment.

Major deaths are required of us each time we are asked to believe in somebody else. Parents, teachers, friends—all know this well. Our transmission of life through actively trusting other human beings depends on our readiness to die to our own concerns or interests. Trust is not the manipulable commodity into which it has been fashioned by psychological gurus in recent years. Trust does not come out of games in which persons are led around blindfolded; it is never so soft or self-indulgent and never so falsely dramatic. Trust is the outcome of transactions in which one person dies to selfishness in order to expand the life and strength of somebody else. It is exactly the same with hope that does not consist in bland good wishes as much as it does in stretching out one's arms to somebody else. Love involves all of these experiences as well as the special death that goes with allowing another person to be separate from us; there is always a death involved as the price of giving someone else a life of their own. Lovers are always freeing each other, accepting the death in separation in order to enrich their love.

That is an old-fashioned idea, but the modern world experiences problems with friendship and death precisely because of its estrangement from such demanding but abiding realities. The best preparation for death is living truly and deeply, being a friend to oneself and to others. Unfortunately, that is sometimes interpreted as throwing oneself into a Zorba-like paroxysm of excess, of trying too hard, in the manner of fiftyish men wearing clusters of beads and animal teeth as though these could ward off the evil spirits of aging and earn them relationships with the young. Living fully does not require doing everything and going everywhere at a dizzying and distracting pace. All we need do is give ourselves to what we do here and now. We need not travel far in order to find the treasures of existence, for they are around us all the time. Any life—even the most ordinary—is crisscrossed by the intersections at which death, linked always to love and friendship, waits to ask us for a sacrifice of ourselves in order that we may make our way more deeply into existence. Death and friendships are natural, the sturdiest fibers of life's great cycle, essential to the grace and strength of its very structure.

Friendship is as important as breathing for us. It is what we are made for, the experience in which we come close to understanding and being ourselves. And it confronts us with death in a thousand small ways all the time. In a sense, friendship tames death because only friendship keeps it in balance. Friendship acquaints us with death, reminds us that we must pass through it and whispers that we are strong enough to survive it.

Friendship causes us, for example, to face our limitations on the one hand and to draw on our spiritual ability to overcome them on the other. We cannot ever completely possess another person, not in the grandest passion or the deepest friendship. There is always a hairline of distance, an elusive protean quality in intimate relationships. It was no accident that making love sexually came to be understood as a "little death." Death grins sardonically at us through the gaps that edge open in every human relationship. Without friendship, without the drive to be as close as possible, we would never feel the sharp ridge of this limitation. Death is on the inside of love—and the deeper the friendship, the greater the pain. Mystery exists within mystery. At the very instant of this potentially depressing insight, friendship gives us the strength, not only to survive, but to commit ourselves anew to closing the fissures that must necessarily be part of human relationships.

The most important business of love and friendship is to hold us together as we live on the shifting edge of our differences. Friendship and love are the life force pitted directly against separation and death at the very core of true intimacy. The trembling edge of our separateness—of our potential estrangement—is the site at which friendship reveals its true power and does its work. Friendship draws us out of ourselves, literally forcing us to draw on faith and hope as we close the fault lines that death would claw wide open in our relationships every day. By being friends we not only hold fast to each other, but we strengthen the forces of life, we overcome death on the battleground of everyday mystery. We are not strangers to death if we are friends with life.

This is not to romanticize death as much as it is to recognize how essential it is for us to live with the great mysteries if we are going to lay hold of our humanity. Neither is it to encourage the false and unnecessary suffering that many people seek and bring upon themselves because they are unwilling to look directly at either life or death. We can only conclude that the problem, as with all mysteries, is simple and insoluble at the same time. We must let ourselves be human and allow the mysteries to be mysteries or we have no way of entering life successfully at all.

FOUR

What Everybody Already Knows About Friendship

Look around you. It isn't just the economy that causes grim faces, the slightly surprised looks on people who have bought cowboy hats or Russian dresses, sniffed a little coke, had a little sex, and still seem unhappy. What they have been looking for cannot be seen in the mirror. Worn out from gazing at themselves and frustrated by the disappointment of the progressive age that was supposed to free them from conflict and guilt, they search for something new that is also something old. They strain, like fighters in a round that seems endless, to hear the bell that will let them out of the ring. They haven't been in good shape since the collapse of the seventies and their promises. What they would really like is something simple, which, after the failure of so many psychological and erotic tricks, really works. They want an experience that is worthy of the complexity of being human.

They are rediscovering friendship.

Friendship, of course, is always being rediscovered.

It is the only safe approach to the experience that has always been stronger even than our oldest mysteries: separation and death. Everybody recognizes friendship, although nobody knows exactly what it is. And everyone surely wants to experience it, although friendship cannot be purchased and withers promptly at the hands of those who try to force it to flower. Friendship is our most familiar mystery, beggaring the Trinity for wonders in our generally ordinary lives. Friendship is our everyday, garden-variety miracle. Through it we all enter the realm of the mystical. Abbots and gurus often say that we cannot enter there unless we change ourselves into something different. Nonsense. We can only enter there as ourselves. Friendship is the best passport to use. When people demand an explanation of the meaning of existence, when they search out the experiences that enable them to get beyond themselves and the mean and bleak stretches of life, they discover that friendship, like spring that waits beneath the ice, provides the most natural and best answer for them. We never enter the mystical dimension of existence by ourselves. A friend has to take us.

They may say otherwise, but everybody bearing the scars of life knows that there is no arcane wisdom and no real secret connected with friendship. The simple truths about friendship and its way of testing and bringing out the best that is in each of us are well and widely known. They come under the heading of hard sayings; we don't learn them easily, but we never forget them. We may not like to think about them, but we nod in recognition when somebody else speaks the truths of friendship out loud. We know, for example, that friends can break our hearts better than anyone else. We know there is a price on friendship. We may

not mind it, but we have to pay it. Friendship is worth
it. Friendship is not like running the four-minute mile.
It is more difficult and more rewarding and it requires
a steady effort rather than a big race. Maybe the best
we can do is to remind people of what they have already learned the hard way and to encourage them to
put this understanding to wise use in their further exploration of friendship. The secret of friendship lies
not in distorting the truth about the subject, but in offering courage to those who know the truth about its
risks and hurts so that they can affirm its presence and
value in their lives.

Friendship is a natural experience. That is why it is
a mystery, too. Such an unadorned appreciation res-
cues it from contrivance and from the promises of the
contemporary hucksters who make successful living
and unlimited happiness seem within one's easy grasp
and control. Synthetic experiences have a lot in common with synthetic fabrics. They don't feel as comfortable as those that are natural. They don't last as long
either.

Friendship is an aspect of an organic reality as natural and as necessary for our human thriving as sun-
shine and fresh air. It is best understood as a part of
the great chain of humanness, the substance that
links us together in the same family. We must respect
its nature and learn to wait for it, as we wait for the
seasons. We must respect its own inner nature and
not falsely manipulate it. We are not Dr. Franken-
steins cranking open the roof of our existence and bidding the lightning to give life to some relationship we
have manufactured out of tricks, social pressures,
emotional bribery, or the flawed innocence of meetings that only seem to happen by accident. Oh, the
awkward arrangements of life! More ingenuity and en-

ergy have gone into trying to make friendship happen that have gone into any other enterprise in the history of the world. If friendship is a natural phenomenon, then nobody can make it happen. One can only listen for and respect the rhythms and moods of its existence and cooperate rather than interfere with them.

That is why friendship remains always to be discovered and why it can never be taken by force. Nobody can seize beauty, peace of mind, or the grandeur of a sunset. Neither can one plant a conqueror's flag in kindness, attention, or the reward of intimacy. These are the gifts we happen onto, most of the time when we are not looking for them, and almost always when we are not thinking of ourselves. Death to the self begets friendship. Forgetting ourselves brings us that freedom—that open space in our entanglements— that makes love possible. That is the moment in which friendship surprises us. Friendship literally catches us off guard—when we are not preening ourselves to make an impression or protecting ourselves from the possibility of truly meeting someone else.

We may be able to prepare ourselves for the sudden gift of friendship, but we can never demand that it be granted us. One of the abiding paradoxes of existence hinges on the conditions for our discovery of friendship: It blossoms naturally in the lives of those who are not looking for it directly; it is the wonderful inheritance of those who understand something about giving themselves away. The sideways discovery, the almost accidental unearthing of friendship—this is the reason for its potent charm.

There are, of course, many things we call friendship that are not friendship at all. Some are second-best arrangements in a cruel world, others a sticky mass of psychological needs that people can't understand or shake loose from. Even though they are neither deep nor lasting enough for that title, some relationships are sorted out under the heading of friendship. But, as with so many things connected with this subject, everybody knows that already.

Indeed, the average person is wise about this subject through observation and experience, some of it hopeful and some of it sad, because we test every relationship, consciously or not, to understand its character and to judge whether it will hold our weight or not. So men and women understand almost intuitively that not everything called friendship deserves that classification. They have a feeling for such things, especially for the false ring of pretended comradeships. They know, most of them firsthand, that people can use each other and not even notice how badly they treat each other. They also understand that people can die of the resulting pain.

What we all understand, better than anything else, about friendship is that, when things go wrong, the results hurt more than any other experience we know. To be wounded in friendship is to be caught in a desert where we cannot shield ourselves from the blinding high-noon sun of betrayal and disappointment. We ache and thirst and can only wait for the pain to wear off and go away. The corruption or loss of friendship is the hell on earth every person dreads. This is the world's open secret about friendship, and everybody—no exceptions—knows about it from personal experience.

But people still seek friendship; they still peer over the guard they raise to protect themselves after previous hurt in order to see if the person approaching might yet be the bearer of the gift of successful friendship. People turn toward friendship the way they naturally seek out other things that are good for them. Just as when, deprived of salt, people seek it out, so by a wisdom of the person that is second cousin to this celebrated wisdom of the body, men and women seek out the company and approval of other persons. They cannot get along without it. Perhaps nothing is more dangerous to the human heart than friendship when it goes wrong; but nothing is better for it when friendship works at least partially right. The best of friendships, after all, exist between people filled with flaws and shortcomings.

Everybody knows that not every friendship is perfect, that, in fact, friendship has little if anything to do with perfection. It occurs only between people who are imperfect; indeed, friendship demands imperfection as a condition for its very existence. Its terrible beauty is born in hazardous circumstances and, small miracle of all homely truths, it thrives in that delicate and shifting space that marks the boundary between people. Friendship grows on the electric currents of exchange between living persons who stand close enough to each other. But they are also close enough to hurt each other worse than anyone else possibly could. That is the terrifying potential in the close quarters of intimacy. The risk of living with the possibility of psychological injury at the hands of friends is inseparable from the experience we call friendship. We simply cannot have one without the other and those who attempt to eliminate the risk of friendship also eliminate the possibility of its occurrence at the same time. Prenuptial contracts designed to eliminate areas of conflict beforehand—such as who will walk the dog and do the dishes, or whose mother-in-law will come for the holidays—are doomed to failure. True friendship is the only thing that can really bear people up in a world in which it is impossible to predict what will go wrong next.

The average person understands that nobody wants deliberately to hurt anybody else and especially not somebody they love. Yet they retain the power to hurt—and exercise it—because they are friends. In a strange and invisible ritual, friends confer that power on each other very early in their relationship so that what the one thinks and feels becomes vitally significant if not decisive to the other. True mutuality gives rise to joy and laughter as well as to the deeper affirmations of identity that are the fruit of a good friendship. But the chance of hurt, even of accidental hurt, is a constant of the environment of human closeness. The wonder of genuine friendship is that it can survive such terrible accidents of the spirit. Friends must understand and overlook each other's faults and mistakes all the time; they are constantly involved in healing each other, in helping each other to get up and carry on in the face of life's constant onslaughts. That is a large part of the business of being friends—sticking with and propping each other up against the world that wants to beat our brains out every day.

What ordinary persons understand about friendship flows from their awareness of the coexistence of the possibility of hurt with the reality of genuine closeness: The blessings and strengths that people give to each other are in proportion to their willingness to run the risk of exposing themselves to hurt, to a death that is sharper than any other. Love's only true measure is our lack of defense in the presence of the beloved. And there is no way, as everyone knows, to plan for or against that.

It is a curious and vexing business, this friendship that is found only in the least likely of places, between the consenting of all ages in the human condition. People do not talk about everything they know of friendship. There is much that must remain unspoken, that does, in fact, go without getting expressed in words even between good friends. That is an aspect of the genius of friendship: It works best when it is least self-conscious, when persons are not trying to show what great friends they are by outdoing each other in sacrifice or periods of long-suffering; friendship does not thrive on such potlatch displays of self-dramatized generosity. It is at its best when friends are so committed to the welfare of the other that they do not count the cost of the attention and time they give to their friend. They are not aware of their own goodness or bravery or steadfastness; they simply respond when they are needed. That truth glows at the core of genuine friendship or love wherever they are found. Friends do not talk about friendship, and those who do, with the excessive sentiment of World War I poets or the bearers of boarding-school crushes, are almost certainly not yet friends in the richest sense of the word.

There are, friends understand, things that are too important to talk about, too easy to destroy or distort by excessive theorizing; there are experiences between people that speak for themselves. One is rightfully suspicious of those who talk too much about friendship or sex; those who understand these subjects never say much about them. That silence is the symbol of the security that is the seal of mature friendship.

Good friends enjoy a treasure not easily described and one that is often denied to the rich and powerful of this world. Since its achievement depends on the simple presence of one person to another, it is often extremely difficult for those who lack simplicity to find real friends. The rich are often so much on their guard against those who curry favor because of their fortune that they cannot lower their defenses to allow true friends to enter their lives. Great wealth, like great beauty, can affect a person's sense of self; he or she may find it impossible to believe that anyone could care for them just for themselves and not for whatever favors they might be able to bestow. So friendship is more often the blessing inherited by the meek and the homely. Blessed are average persons for theirs is the kingdom of friendship.

Friendship, as a matter of fact, makes defenses unnecessary. Far more surely than the tricks of psychological self-puffery, friendship allows persons to be themselves. When friends are together they need assume no airs and strike no poses that do not reflect their own truth. Friendship creates the world in which we can comfortably be ourselves, in which we are valued above all things for that, and in which we need not strive to make some other impression to win favor or approval. It is a small gift, the free and unforced approval of a friend, and yet, more than any other, it makes a truthful and purposeful human life possible. Friends, in the best sense of the term, are disarming; they take away our need for weapons so that we can stand without hiding our blemishes and shortcomings in the light of a relationship that is strong enough to make these flaws evident and cause them to pale into relative insignificance at the same time.

Another thing everybody knows is that other persons have more friends than they do. The other side of this coin of delusion is that we imagine that other people do not have troubles. There is some comfort in the realization that we are all so pressed by life that we share this same distortion. Friendship, however, is not something that others have in abundance while we, waiflike and lonely, stand vulnerable before an unforgiving and unfriendly world. That sense of loneliness, that feeling that one's friends may be true but few, that daily oppression that arises because of so many obligations to meet, so many tests of one kind or another to pass long after we have left school, is one of our most common human experiences, something we all feel. There is, indeed, a special poignancy about how widely this experience is shared; it is something that enables us to recognize each other as brothers and sisters in the same big family and to understand our smallness and how frightened we are of the possible shattering of the fragile bonds that hold us together. Such an insight, through which we recognize how much we truly share, gives us a vision of our common need, a sense of how each day we all rise to face similar difficulties with hearts that need friendship and that may be broken in its quest. And we all know about that.

The homely poetry of such understandings prepares us to review some of the great themes connected with friendship, to see them more humanly and naturally, and perhaps with a greater readiness to be more understanding and friendly to each other. One cannot think about friendship long without becoming a better friend to the world of people around us. We are about to explore what most of us already know, not to expose it to excessive analysis, but to recognize our common birthright to friendship and to use that as a basis for its understanding and extension in our lives.

FIVE

Face to Face with Ourselves

WE would be surprised to learn how many people are not comfortable with themselves. No, we wouldn't be surprised. We have often caught at least a glimpse through squinted eyes at our own less desirable characteristics. We wince, the way we did as children when our parents told embarrassing infancy stories, when we think about how foolish, impulsive, or self-centered we can sometimes be, and of how we can hurt others and ourselves at the same time. We are sometimes ashamed of that person who lives with us, the skeleton in the closet of our identity, that double-agent who allows us, without even taking a swig of the steamy elixir, to see our conflicted selves in the story of Dr. Jekyll and Mr. Hyde.

How, we ask, can we be friendly with parts of us we don't like, parts of us we don't even want to get to know?

It is not easy. Neither is it as hard as it is sometimes made out to be. Getting on better terms with ourselves is a lifelong task. There are no overnight cures, no transformations over a weekend at some therapy spa. Being on good terms with ourselves is an essential predisposition to the making of successful friendships with other people. Nowhere does the Bible tell it more accurately than in its injunction to love our neighbor as we love ourselves. If we love our neighbors at all, we do it very much in the way in which we love ourselves. The game plan for getting on with other people is clearly outlined in our mode of getting on with ourselves.

The information that comes out of our relationships with others allows us to take an indirect but informative look at the way we treat ourselves. That is helpful, since ordinarily most of us who are reasonably free of masochism do not like to examine our faults. We wish that someone else—anybody else—would do the work for us. Hence the self-help industry, a multinational operation that profits from human misery. Self-help books are actually misnamed. They do not even suggest that we help ourselves; their whole point is that their authors are going to help us and that we can take their word for our decisions about everything from making love to making money. The whole enterprise of self-help is an illusion designed to make the manipulator of our lives invisible, thus leaving us with the idea that we are the captains of our own souls. This is wonderful stuff, most of it related to salesmanship, bottles of dark liquid for a dollar off the backs of wagons. Its modernized form seems sophisticated, but it is still the old pitchman capitalizing on our fears and uneasiness and providing us with connect-the-dots plans for hugely successful lives. The trouble with us is that we have taken self-help books so seriously. You would think they were diet books. Only when we smile indulgently at them can we understand that they are symptoms of rather than solutions to our distress. They are written mostly by people unacquainted with mystery and unfamiliar with the true depths of either friendship or death.

There is an easier and more human way. Our most reliable knowledge about how we look at and treat ourselves comes from an inspection of the way we treat the people closest to us. If we are overbearing and always anxious to keep others under our control, we can be sure that we treat ourselves the same way. If we are suspicious of the motives of those around us, we do not trust ourselves much either. Staying aloof and emotionally cool has been a popular contemporary stance; that only means that great numbers of us stay at an uninvolved distance from ourselves. We wish to be innocent bystanders in the events of our lives, but that does not lessen our discomfort with our own personalities. It just keeps us from ever discovering the roots of our uneasiness and of doing anything about them.

People who get through life by manipulating others also play tricks on themselves. The pain that bubbles just below the level of such adjustments would provide, were it retrievable (imagine an immense drilling rig on the sea of our distress), the solution to the world's energy problems. There is no shortage of the suffering that goes with not really knowing or liking oneself. And many people try everything but the simple, direct method in order to know and to help themselves. For example, many urban Western people seek peace by transforming themselves into Eastern mystics. It usually wears off after a while.

For example, men and women often live in the third person. They run their lives as though they were directing and measuring their growth from a wrinkled set of blueprints handed to them by some snarling foreman. The specifications are all there, but they are in somebody else's handwriting. They follow them because they are afraid of the foreman, whether he is God, parents, or the boss. Individuals trapped in this kind of adjustment live with too much dependence on the aphorisms and instructions of others. It does not matter whether these suggestions are those of a righteous preacher, the *Playboy* "Advisor" or some *Cosmo* incarnation of Helen Gurley Brown. Living through the advice of another is not the same as living in and through a man or woman's own identity. Those who make the suggestions usually do so with the best of intentions: They want to help others live more successfully and happily. But providing behaviors from the outside that will supposedly win others acclaim and popularity may well undermine their self-confidence and make it more difficult for them to know themselves firsthand and, therefore, to be themselves comfortably.

In other words, formulas applied to life may seem to lead to "successful" activity, particularly through the assumption of currently acceptable beliefs or ways of living that win the approval of others. People who cut their heads to fit these hats may also estrange themselves from their true characteristics and interests because the positions shaped for them by others make it hard for them to see what they really look like. Such behaviors can be as varied as jumping into bed as quickly as possible with new acquaintances, ordering the right wines, or selecting a career in computer technology. When a man or woman makes a decision principally because "a modern person does this" or "a macho man does this," that person may be following stage directions written for somebody else.

Acting doesn't get us through life. Many actors confess they do not know what to say unless someone else writes words for them. They live in the third person, on the promptings of strangers with wit. The life of the play is not their own, no matter how fully they give themselves to their roles. They remove their makeup and go home after each performance to what they know as "real life." For many of them, however, the feeling of being alive only comes when they are performing. Stars who survive communicate directly with the public because they possess definable personalities of their own; these genuine features of their character transcend the roles written for them. People go to see them be themselves. That is why they admire them.

In life, however, people who live in the third person are already in "real life." As the man in the *New Yorker* cartoon told his little girl when their car had a flat in the rain, "I can't change the channel. This is life." There is no place to go after the performance except to lonely rooms. They cannot change the world or themselves because they have not learned to value sufficiently the truths about themselves; they do not think the truth will be good enough to get by with. They prefer a pseudotruth to the facts about themselves. They cannot easily say "I"—about their preferences, "I like"; about their religious beliefs, "I believe"; of their political convictions, "I vote for." It is no wonder that they melt into the mass of persons around them, that they can seem indistinguishable from all the others who tread water in social existence with the same ideas and opinions.

They are not, in short, friends with themselves. This problem in relating to themselves causes them to have problems in relating to others. As with themselves, so they are with others. It is a miserable not a sinful state, all too human and recognizable. Such men and women need encouragement to be themselves rather than prefabricated personalities supplied by others; they need to come to terms with the truths that finally will make them free and open the world of friendship for them.

Some supposedly religious leaders have thumped away at the idea of judgment day as the time at which we and all our secrets will be laid bare. We shall stand around on something like a stadium field covering ourselves as modestly as possible, unglued at the prospect of all our thoughts and actions being exposed to the onlookers—a superbowl of shame with grinning devils as cheerleaders. What an abiding theme in certain theological discourse! And all this from those who tell us that God is love.

Every day is judgment day for too many people. They tremble at the prospect of others getting to know their true selves; they will surely be abandoned or condemned when the truth comes out. This is another aspect of the truly dreadful theology that has made people aware of their failings and afraid that, sooner or later, they will be found out. The religio-social leverage of guilt and unworthiness in our lives has certainly contributed to the difficulties many people have in identifying and respecting their own personalities. That is one of the reasons for the perennial success of the hawkers of easy redemption for those weighed down with anxiety about their own worth. Away with this judgment-day scenario, as well as all quick cures for our sorrowful state! We make progress when we can adopt the only viewpoint worthy of Divinity: understanding and compassion for our human situation.

Take Jehovah's view of our condition for a moment: not some thundering God out for vengeance and not an English butler of a God whose attention we cannot get despite our prayers and worship. Suppose God were as understanding as the most understanding person you ever met, the one who made you feel at ease and did not shame you, the man or woman who was able to accept your human frailty and restore hope and courage to you. Such people exist, as we all know. They keep the world going at those moments when it threatens to collapse; they help us to survive because they neither approve nor disapprove of our weakness, but they profoundly understand it.

This is not a romantic notion. We can all be understanding if we take the time to learn the facts and the infinite complications of the lives of people all around us. André Malraux wrote of the army chaplain priest who, when asked what he had learned from his many years of hearing confessions, replied that most men were just children. We need a healthy, not to say earthy, feeling for our struggles in order to come to terms with ourselves and the diverse aspects of our personalities, ranging from our tempers to our sexuality. When judgment day comes, God, of all things, is going to be understanding. He is going to let us see the truth about ourselves, that wonderful freeing truth that survives beneath our posturings, our ambitions, and our exaggerated ideas about ourselves. Seeing that truth whole is judgment enough; it also saves us.

To understand all, the old saying goes, is to forgive all. What redeems us in our human existence is our capacity to see into people with compassion for their lives. There is nothing more poignant or stirring than human beings struggling against odds and disadvantages to make a good and decent life. Power resides in the truth uttered by human beings who will, if we give them a chance, face it and tell it about themselves. Our ability to face the mischance and evil of life truthfully is one irrefutable measure of our maturity. To be able to understand how adolescent most of us are at least some of the time is the human faculty that finally makes us lovable.

That simple kind of understanding—the kind God, if He truly is God, must possess—is what we need to treat ourselves as subjects rather than objects in life. Compassion is the basis of friendship with ourselves. Judgment day is every day anyway and, in any given twenty-four hours, most of us make so many mistakes that we would be depressed permanently if we lacked the capacity to understand. That capacity allows us to see into ourselves—into our unretouched souls, into ourselves as we really are—and not be frightened by the sight.

When we can see enough to be touched by the utter humanity of our good points and bad features, when we can, in other words, acknowledge that we are nothing more and nothing less than human, we achieve a secure basis for a longlasting friendship with ourselves. We pass through a death and come out alive. At the same time, we establish a firm foundation for friendship with other persons. That is because we have learned to let the truth—our truth—show through our pretensions. We have let something die and we have found life. We have loosed the person who can truly be friends with others on the world.

Of course, we must be watched.

SIX

Being Friendly to Ourselves

WATCHING ourselves need not be a vain exercise, as it often is when we check our appearance in mirrors or store windows. It does not need to be as painful as it is when we confront our undeniable shortcomings and our occasional nastiness. Watching ourselves can, in fact, be quite bearable when, fortified with a sense of humor, we make our observations from the mature heights of our personalities. The capacity to watch ourselves wth humane understanding well seasoned with irony is an indisputable sign of our sanity. It is also first-class evidence that we have a good friendship with ourselves.

A sympathetically detached view of ourselves in motion in life is essential for contentment as well as for developing and deepening our relationships with others. Far truer than even Murphy's law is this one: If we are friendly to ourselves, others will be friendly to us. Watching ourselves, then, is not a self-conscious desire to make sure we have our hair in place or that we are wearing the latest fashion in an appropriately casual way. Self-observation has nothing to do with the way we look. It focuses on the way we are. Ordinary language is filled with phrases that describe well the man and woman who are able to see themselves clearly in the context of life. There is, in other words, no secret about this apparent secret of happy living. People look in many directions for the formula for success. They buy a lot of psychological patent medicine that they don't need. The truth lies literally within themselves. They just have to learn how to get a good look at it.

People commonly speak of healthy individuals as those who don't take themselves too seriously. We all know that sensible men and women are able to laugh at themselves. They live in the real world, we say, and they can see things, including themselves, as they are. All these homely phrases bubble up from a fund of good sense that has been slowly and painfully accumulated through the human misadventures we call history. Knowing ourselves perennially has been considered essential to the good life, and we pay the highest compliment to others when we say that they don't fool themselves or, more simply, that they are themselves. You wouldn't think it would be so rare, would you?

The happy life—the life graced with friendship—is not so much a story of people overcoming every obstacle as it is of their living contentedly within their limitations. Friendship with the self and with others depends on a clear-eyed understanding of the boundaries of the human situation, of the fact that we cannot have everything, that we must learn to make room for each other, that death waits like a hooded judge for each one of us, that, in fact, something about the briefness of our days, the slight cast of the shadows of even the greatest among us, makes friendship the most natural of our inclinations and the most human of our achievements. Friendship is not just some elaboration of the herd instinct. Considering the cramped space and the faulted conditions of life, it is the most remarkable accomplishment of the human spirit. We can reach across the distance between us and support and enlarge each other; we can overcome our bewildered estrangement at being on this planet together through friendship. Take a look at our collective being slogging forward through the centuries. How familiar this talent for affiliation. How like us, we might say in pleased astonishment, to recognize our longing for friendship.

We know, individually, that we have transforming moments in everyday life when we get a glimpse of this urge. There are times when we catch ourselves doing the right thing by each other. We may shrug them off or deny them, or plead state's evidence—good men and women often do that—but those instances in which we are true and generous, in which we surrender something of ourselves for the sake of others, are the luminous signals of our positive capacity for relationships. We should take hope and courage from them.

How, then, do we make self-observation a more systematic and effective part of our lives? Can we learn to see ourselves in action on better than a random basis? Insight should be more than accidental and, with patience and understanding, we can make it so. We may begin by noticing those moments during which we clearly, if briefly, see the truth about ourselves. These may be times when we regret some move we have made, when, for example, we feel bad that we lost our temper in a situation that did not call for such a strong reaction, when we saw a flash of the demon who ordinarily lives quietly within us.

It is not uncommon for persons to say something like this: "Boy, I did a dumb thing today," or "I really blew it," or "I acted like a child this afternoon." Sometimes the message to ourselves is not that clear. We need to overhear ourselves as, for example, when we notice that we are bragging a lot about some accomplishment, or when we seem to be badly in need of attention, or when we insist on our viewpoint more stridently than usual. At times we just have a vague feeling of uneasiness about our behavior. We get fed up with ourselves.

Consider a common and trivial example, the footnote kind of experience that occurs thousands of times each day. We are driving to or from work and we become angry with another motorist. We may, in that situation, do things that do not seem characteristic of us. We may use language and gestures—the vulgar street theater of the eighties—that we would hardly employ anywhere else. And we may growl and complain and defend ourselves vigorously if our driving companion—particularly if it is a spouse—suggests that we may have been partially at fault. We defend ourselves, sometimes hotly, and it is only as the incident cools and recedes that we may admit that we were mistaken in our judgment and that our excessive insistence on being right was really a defensive indication of how wrong we were.

Everyone has gone through experiences like that. What is important for us to locate is that observation post on the self from which we can look back at our mistake and understand the pattern of our own exaggerated self-protection. The lookout is anchored in the mature part of our personality, the ego, as the experts call it, from which we watch the ebb and flow of our unconscious strivings. The ego is a kind of conning tower that allows us to chart the tides of our less mature selves—sometimes the child, sometimes the adolescent, and at other times the seemingly deranged inhabitant, the crazy uncle of our personality who only occasionally gets out of the attic but causes quite a scare when he does. These varied performers are not, however, demonic presences any more than our dreams are cable television for the mind. When we observe this striking cast of characters, we watch the many faces of our own complexity, the Mr. Hydes within us all. We may not like what we see, we may close our eyes and shudder, or we may try to walk indignantly out of the theater and get our money back. All to no avail. What we see, as the saying goes, is what we get and, we might add, what we also give in our relationships to others. It is small wonder that human beings, aware of the strangeness of their own behavior over the centuries, have believed that outside forces, devils or spells, could explain the behavior that arises from the many-tiered structure of their own selves.

Persons who are friendly to themselves do, in situations like this, what good friends always do. They do not condemn or turn away; they listen and try, even when it is difficult, to understand. The self we observe may be engaged in behavior far more puzzling than that cited in the example of traffic jam temper. The capacity to observe remains the same and the effort to understand, as a friend would, is essential. If, for example, we allow our defenses to collapse of their own weight, we can inspect the incident more carefully. We begin to track down the underlying causes of what appeared to be an untypical piece of behavior.

The will to understand leads us to ask gentle questions about ourselves. Getting on better terms with our own personalities does not flow from looking away from what we have done or claiming that everything that happens to us is somebody else's fault. Friendship with ourselves, like friendship anywhere, depends on simple honesty. This is not the ruthless honesty of a prosecuting attorney but the easy honesty of those who are comfortable in dealing with the truth. What kinds of questions does this prompt us to ask?

The observing self, in the situation described, would want to understand the emotional energy beneath the reaction. Tracing our emotions to their origins always brings us closer to the truth about ourselves. Why did I get so angry? Why did I speak and make gestures that are not part of my usual behavior? Are they expressive of some part of me that I usually do not notice or do not wish to notice? Am I angry at something else in my life? Is the anger from that source erupting— and thereby revealing its strength—in minor incidents in which I let strangers bear the brunt of feelings that have nothing to do with them? Is my discontent really centered on work, marriage, or some failure to come to terms with my own self?

The questions lead from one to another and bring us quickly down that long hallway to the truth that, in a complicated and surprising way, had asserted itself in the afternoon traffic. We need not treat ourselves harshly to discover this truth. We mine it out of ourselves gradually as we sift through the layers of our reactions. By this means we reach the column of truth that finally must support our lives. When our observing self sees that truth with understanding, we automatically strengthen our internal friendship. Such understanding makes it possible for us to modify our behavior by identifying its genuine roots—in this case, the source of our anger—and dealing more forthrightly with them. The simple acknowledgment of such truth is the beginning of wisdom, the start of more adult behavior on our part. We face the facts and we are not destroyed by the encounter. The power they hold over us when they remain in the dark is considerably weakened when we bring these things into the light. We may not like what we see, but we are better off seeing it than being blind to our true motivations and living by defensive maneuvers. Again, by facing a death about ourselves, we stake a stronger claim on life. We are distinctly unfriendly to ourselves when we allow unconscious conflicts to rule our lives and when, as a result, we hide not only the truth about ourselves, but the truth about our other relationships.

Observing ourselves must not be confused with the anxious "watching" of the self that can plague people. Anxiety about one's appearance or one's performance, the warm and uneasy weight of shyness—these experiences are quite different from mature self-examination. These are important human signals from the growing part of ourselves, observable feelings rather than well-made observations in themselves.

These self-conscious resonations can cause great pain and suffering for those whose freedom is compromised by them. Like other feelings that flow from conflicted or undeveloped aspects of our personalities, these need to be noted and explored by the adult ego. Listening to oneself may seem an arduous or boring task; it is, however, an essential condition of growing in friendship with oneself. Hearing what we are saying and noticing what we are doing does not make us suffocatingly preoccupied or pompous. Self-observation is at its best a light and graceful activity, a source of revitalization that keeps us well grounded in our lives and our work. Watching and learning from the self may take a measure of courage and integrity, but it is never boring and it leads, in the long run, to good things like contentment and peace of mind. Sensible self-observation—an easy monitoring of ourselves—saves us from a great deal of pain, especially from the almost intractable variety that goes with snarled human relationships.

There may be few ailments of the human spirit more devastating than emotional involvements, the entanglements to which no man or woman who has lived very long is a stranger. There is no way to avoid this particular hazard of living; there are, however, ways to endure and survive it successfully. These depend on our capacity for accurate self-observation.

The symptoms of emotional involvement are well known. They may be clinically observed in a highly virulent state in the crushes of the adolescent years. The fever of emotional involvement may continue long after that developmental period has been concluded. It is accompanied by intense preoccupation wth the person of the other and the many reactions associated with this. Obsession may not be too strong a word for the emotional absorption that is the essence of the experience. What is the other person doing? That is the recurrent question during any periods of separation from the beloved. This leads to awkward expressions of concern, numerous phone calls, notes, mountains of failed poetry, and manifest inattention to the duties of work or study that are at hand. Meetings that are supposed to be accidental are arranged with as much care as was invested in the Normandy landings.

The heart aches, the soul pines, the head reels: You'll know it when you see it.

There is nothing unusual about this involvement. It is natural even though the person caught up in it may call it spiritually transcendent one moment and the devil's own work the next.

The watching and listening to the self that allows us to pass through the ordeal of emotional involvement is not done just with our eyes or our intellects. We observe with our whole adult personality, catching the meaning of the situation with our intellects but letting its impact register in our own emotions as well. The observations we make are of what we do or say, of its emotional roots, and of our reactions as we watch in retrospect. This may seem complex, but it is only so in describing what, for many, is an intuitive human process. We listen with our whole selves to anything that is of vital concern to us; we pay attention to those we truly love and we may, in fact, relish every sensation associated with certain relationships. That full attention is what we give, out of friendship for ourselves, to the range of reactions we experience in emotional involvements.

Such listening does not heal us completely, but it does give us the foundation on which we can stand and from which we can view what is happening to us. Self-observation gives us a quiet place in the storm of feelings that may accompany tangled interpersonal relationships. Self-observation helps because the fundamental causes of confusion in overheated relationships are unconscious. We listen for the rumblings that tell the deep origins of the feelings that seem to draw us willy-nilly into intimacy with others. The role of our own psychological life history as it intersects with that of another person is crucial. We project onto others needs whose origins lie deep inside ourselves. We are sometimes attracted in profound and truly irrational ways to people whose own inner conflicts match, as one jigsaw piece does another, our own. The tumult of the attraction and the intensity of the experience are counterpointed by the grinding pain of the disillusionment that occurs when the seizure passes. Men and women feel crushed by the disappointments of what appears to be love and then turns out to be something altogether different. They stagger away from such relationships like wounded soldiers from a battlefield. They even vow that they will never allow themselves to get into such relationships again. The households of America are littered with the aftermath of these relationships.

Observing the self allows persons, first of all, to sense something of their own conflicts or psychological needs. That side-of-the-eye inspection of our own emotional pull and drag provides us with a reading of our reactions to others. We can tell, if we are honest, when the adolescent side of our personality is asserting itself. That is a help in relating to others because it signals the role of distortion and need. When the needle passes a certain point we can understand—and we may even assent to it for the moment—that our immature self is having the upper hand in a certain relationship. The adult ego saves itself a great deal of anguish by exercising some moderating control over these impulses. That is the first step in dealing in a healthy and human way with our friendships. Knowing what we are getting into—and not fooling ourselves about it—is a friendly act toward our own personalities.

There is no way, of course, to eliminate tangled and hurting emotional relationships from our lives. Persons who lay back from all relationships in order to protect themselves from ever being hurt may succeed in numbing themselves to such harm. They also damage their friendship with themselves in the process. The pullback from the possibility of being burned by a close relationship gone wrong is a failure to love the self properly, a refusal to believe in or to trust one's own being. It is a sure invitation to continual psychological discomfort and loneliness. That is no way to work out the challenge of being enough in relationship to the self to allow it to face the chanciness that is always involved in making friends with others.

We may not be able completely to cure the wounds of emotional involvements and we certainly cannot avoid social living as a precaution against such injury. As with so many other aspects of the glittering mystery of existence, we can learn to live wisely with the challenge. Listening gently and attentively to what transpires in our own emotional lives is the means we use to attend properly to our fundamental relationships with ourselves. Even beginning to establish diplomatic relationships with ourselves—being able to listen once in a while—improves our own inner friendship. This better-developed sense of ourselves permits us to move more securely into the world of other people. We are not always in danger of being overwhelmed; we need not fear the blind loss of our hearts to those who may manhandle them. We can move among other men and women and not have our own integrity always at stake. Because we don't need to prove ourselves, or our wisdom, or our sexual prowess, or anything else to others, we will be more relaxed and able to enjoy our relationships more freely. Friendship with the self, which depends on monitoring our inner lives with understanding, may not eliminate painful emotional involvements; but through it we can understand what happens to us in our tangled relationships and find our way out without permanent damage to our souls. It helps us face death in life and not be destroyed by it.

SEVEN

Being Friendly to Others

THERE is no survival without ironic objectivity about ourselves. It is the surprising source of salvation for those of us—how vast our number—who would otherwise die of impacted self-consciousness and pompousness, holding doggedly to distorted views of ourselves, puzzled and hurt at the giggling world's failure to accept them. Being objective about ourselves does not demand a cold clinical assessment of our strengths and weaknesses. Essentially friendly, human objectivity also begets friendliness and permits us to see ourselves as part of the great disorganized parade of men and women doing their best against the odds that existence lays down against them every day.

We are grand and foolish at the same time, something like Jerry Ford on his first morning as president of the United States when the camera caught him as he appeared in his short summer pajamas to pluck the morning newspaper off his front porch. We smile warmly at the human quality of the former president's action; we can also smile forgivingly at much of what we ourselves do every day. How human, we say, how very human. Friendship with the self, that strong foundation for friendship with others, depends on the daily rediscovery of our simple humanity.

This viewpoint allows us to understand our failures and shortcomings even when we do not condone or settle carelessly for them. Irony also makes it safe for us to inspect our strengths; otherwise it would be dangerous to look at our good points and we might fly too close to the sun of our own fascination or tumble into the shimmering pool of our narcissism. Distance is necessary even for appraisal and a proper use of our strengths. Only this space enables us to perceive them accurately and not to become intoxicated with the possibilities of our own grandeur.

Truly talented people are hardly ever self-conscious about their ability; they do not work as though they were press agents for their own genius. Their forgetfulness of themselves in whatever task they give themselves to—art, sports, teaching, or caring for others —flows from their basic respect for themselves. Respect comes from a Latin word that means "to look at again." People who are truly talented have looked again at themselves; they have viewed themselves with enough objectivity to do right by themselves and to take healthy risks with themselves and their abilities in life.

Men and women who are friendly with themselves do not need gaudy banners to remind them that the achievements of love and work demand risks. Deep within themselves they understand this truth without putting it into words; they appreciate the fact that they would shrivel and die, that they would not be true to themselves at all, unless they risked the capital of their personalities every day. Such lovers and workers are not reckless individuals who lack an understanding of what they are doing. Because they have an ironic appreciation of themselves, they understand quite well that they may fail or be misunderstood; because they have learned to be friends with themselves, they live with a knowledge that life may hurt them unexpectedly at any time. This tragic sense is not the same thing as a clinical depression. It is a necessary aspect of friendliness with ourselves and with the world of strangers around us; friendliness balances itself with a realistic appreciation for the nature of men and women and is not deluded by images of human nature that are either too easy or too stark.

Human beings are not noble savages or totally depraved creatures. They are somewhere in between. A mature sense of the faulted state that we all share enlivens rather than depresses us. Only those who know how much there is to lose can understand how much there is to gain in confronting the essential mysteries of love and death that lift off the soul of friendship. Our relationships are not accidental. They are never, in fact, merely casual. When we touch each other even slightly on the long voyage of life, we leave marks of one kind or another. We are better or worse, more or less, because of our contacts with each other. The whole design of our existence flows from the model of relationship that we fashion first with ourselves and then with others.

When we speak of friendship, then, we deal with a phenomenon that carries the mark of our souls and holds the meaning of our lives. We discover our significance as we work out the mystery that begins with meeting and that grows, as a tree might, in and through the way we live with and learn to love each other. People are not to be sentimentalized, as they can be in advertisements from the phone company that wants you to use its long-distance service to "reach out and touch" somebody. Neither are others to be used, as they are in a narcissistic age, principally for self-gratification. Sometimes people are used for pseudospiritual reasons by others who see them as those to whom good can be done in order to achieve a heavenly reward for doing good. But people are too important and tough, too absolutely vital just as they are, for us to treat them that way. Friendship depends on relating to ourselves and others for intrinsic reasons. We don't have to manufacture a motive for responding to each other. It is humanly fitting.

When we reflect on friendship, we are concerned, not with something extra, not with some lucky break in life, but with the experience that naturally defines and gives us meaning. Working out our relationships is the work of life; meeting their demands is the measure of our moral outlook; friendship, in any and all of its branching forms, is what life is all about. We humans have a talent for and an attraction to mystery that at one moment leaps out at us and at another hides shyly from us. We see it in love and death, in birth and growth, and in a hundred other hints about its majesty. Friendship is the common path that leads us into life's very heart.

An awareness of the dimensions of friendship may be essential to rescue men and women from the trivialized position in which they find themselves in mass society. Friendship is the tiny whispering sound after the earthquake and fire, the soft invitation that brought the biblical Elijah out of the cave in which he had taken shelter. *Relationship*—that much-abused word—is not a whirlwind but a soft breeze; when we hear it, we can give up the shelter of our own selfishness and discover life. It is profoundly ironical that those who seek to master life by being number one, by winning above all else, often seem hurt and confused—and desperately lonely—when the mighty noise of their self-centeredness turns into a hollow echo. Yet those who see friendship as the path of life are faced with liking themselves enough to be able to put themselves aside for the sake of others, to give up wanting to be number one. Men and women who are friendly to themselves learn, of all things, to let go of themselves for the sake of believing in and loving others.

A mighty power resides in the persons who know how to be friends. They can enlarge the lives of others, they can heal their wounds, they can see them through the most complex of problems in order to achieve the simplest of rewards—honor and truth and integrity, the sense of lives well lived. They also do this for themselves. We become heroes by being friends. We frequently do not observe this hero inside us as clearly as we do the wrongdoer or the self-concerned adolescent in ourselves. One of the great mysteries of life lies in the fact that people so regularly fail to see, or deliberately look away from, what is good about themselves. Born for friendship and at our best in the midst of it, we treat ourselves in an unfriendly manner.

Such unkindness to ourselves! We have all noticed it. We have even taken a certain perverse delight in it. As if that were not bad enough, we often shrink back from or make little of what is best about ourselves. The impulse to friendship must be very deep for us to overcome all the obstacles we place in its way. It is not at all unusual, for example, for persons to deny that they can play the piano after they have taken lessons for ten years, or to deny that they can speak French after a similar period of study. Sometimes they deny that they are capable of tenderness. Hanging back, some men and women do not let themselves or others see what they are good at. Standing at the edge of the crowd replaces joining in the music, silence sounds more loudly for them than speech, and a macho presentation of the self overwhelms their spontaneous gentleness. Sometimes it takes an emergency to bring these good things out of us.

Two questions occur to those interested in being friends. First, why do we cover up what is good about us when we don't work nearly so hard at masking what is bad in us? After all, people are always telling us what is wrong with us. There appears to be no secret about our faults; even strangers or new acquaintances feel free to tell us about them. Second, why is it that our strengths need to be discovered by others, almost by accident? "I saw something in you I never saw before," a friend will say, and we may then let ourselves see it for the first time.

If we watch ourselves at all, we know that we treat ourselves poorly when we obscure our strengths, when we make it harder for others to find and appreciate them. This shyness about our good qualities is a charming puzzle about human nature. It is, however, one of the things that makes us endearing and lovable. Astonishingly, this quirk, this fault line in ourselves, makes us vulnerable to friendship; our strengths, standing just in the shadow of our flaws, can be called forth by someone else. Once out in the open, a good quality can slip back only clumsily out of sight.

Friendship cannot be defined easily. People know what the idea means and they know it when they experience it, but the wisest philosophers have come up with only approximations of friendship's true nature.

That, of course, is natural for any of the mysteries that pervade our existence. Nobody has ever given a satisfactory definition of love, art, or loneliness. Even the doctors disagree violently about defining death. These experiences are, in a sense, far too sacred and significant for us to allow anybody else to define them for us anyway. We must, if we are to pass the initiation ceremonies of a truly human life, enter these mysteries and find out what they are like for ourselves. They may look slightly different every time we commit ourselves to them. That, too, reveals something about their nature.

If we cannot offer a fully satisfying description of friendship, we can, like great travel writers, convey the mood and texture of our passages through relationships with others. We do not usually succeed by directly seeking friendship. Is there anything more poignant than the personal ads (Seeking woman companion, thirty to forty, to share interest in art, good music, dancing) or the promises of computer dating? We ordinarily stumble into friendship the way we stumble into love. It may seem like an accident, although closer inspection often shows that we have been getting ready to have just such an accident for years. Friends are prepared to recognize each other by a long life history of sharing experiences, by events and relationships that bring friends ever closer to each other without their being aware of it. This remote preparation for meeting and recognizing each other is one of the largely unexplored truths about friendship. If, however, we observe our lives carefully, we can discern the slowly converging paths of interests and activities that bring us finally face to face with the person we call a friend.

Friendship affects our vision so that we do see something about another person that signals the possibility of friendship. Friends constantly improve and enlarge each other's vision. It is commonplace for persons to describe the effects of friendship in terms of sight. "I never saw myself this way before," they will report, or "I know that I look different now." Friendship influences perception profoundly. We see things that we were never able to see before, both in our friend, ourselves, and in the great world around us. What was once drab and uninteresting is suddenly suffused with wonder. The routine activities of life take on a magic that we never suspected they could possess. We not only see more, but we also enjoy more and feel better about ourselves. The universe appears different because friendship has struck the restrictive blinders from our eyes. We can see more for a good reason: We are looking now at the world with someone else. We should expect to see more. That is one of the signs of a healthy friendship, just as a diminishing of our view, a turning in on ourselves in a relationship, suggests that such an experience cannot be friendship at all.

Friendship is not blind any more than love is. It actually enables us to see more of each other and of our universe. Friendship does not, however, permanently idealize the other. Any relationship in which false glamorization of the other persists needs careful observation because such continuing distortion is not characteristic of genuine friendship. Thinking well of another does not mean that we see them as lacking all imperfection. Friends come to identify and understand each other's flaws and shortcomings. That is a vital aspect of a realistic and mature friendship. Seeing more of each other, we also understand better the nature and origin of what is immature about each other. Friendship makes our observing self more subtle, exact, and sympathetic. We discover, in Saul Bellow's wonderful phrase, that we all have the "universal eligibility to be noble."

Friendship is a process in which the ore of our humanity is sifted and refined so that the strengths may be reinforced and the weaknesses may be gradually neutralized. True friends bring out the best that is in each other, not in some jolly, backslapping manner, nor in some grim, confrontational style. Freeing our better qualities is a natural occurrence, much as is the release of the potential of the newly planted seed by sun and water. It is the kind of thing that happens when persons grow close to each other, breaking through the suffocating mask of their own containment as they do. There are no tricks involved, no human-potential gimmicks, no self-conscious acts of the will. Let people become friends and this mutual-growth process inevitably follows.

Men and women become themselves through friendship. They find in this relationship the place where they can stand without the supports or affectations they may previously have used to impress others or to conceal their defects. Being themselves does not signify that friends can be rude, sloppy, and inconsiderate of each other and get away with it. In friendship they free themselves from the selfishness through which they may formerly have imposed on others with the claim that they were just being themselves. Friends allow us to bring to life that better self that we may have kept mysteriously hidden. They allow us to pierce the boundaries of the defenses that have forced us to hold back out of fear that, if others get a good look at us, they might not like us any more.

Friendship is the antidote to the varieties of fear that poison our lives. Fear prevents the birth of the real person who struggles beneath layers of shyness and intimidation. Only friendship provides the environment in which it is safe for the genuine personality to step forward confidently. The shrouds of cloth that obscure the richness of the individual drop away as they do at the unveiling of a painting so that we can at last see the beauty that has been hidden. This is a reciprocal process so that friends, at the very same time, free each other from the false burdens of defenses. Friendship with ourselves leads to friendship with others. This, in turn, deepens our relationship with ourselves. That is the indefinable core of the mystery of friendship.

EIGHT

The Work of Friendship

"MARRIAGES," the celebrated columnist Ann Landers once wrote, "may be made in heaven, but the maintenance work goes on down here on earth." One of the grittier truths—how else could they match us humanly?—about the great mysteries in which our lives are set is that they do not take care of themselves. One of the most tragic misunderstandings about our richest experiences is that they somehow possess us from without. People speak of love as something outside themselves; they wonder if love will ever "come along," or if they will "find it" someday. People speak of death as a black-cloaked visitor, a horseman stalking out of an Ingmar Bergman movie, always a stranger speaking a language we have never heard before. So it is with evil when we objectify it as an external force that takes possession of us; so it is when we look for deliverance from our troubles through friendly visitors from other planets; so it is whenever we expect somebody else to save us.

None of these mysteries exist if we do not work at

them from the inside. Mystery is an interaction, just as a poem is, between a person and the star-crossed universe. Just as friendship cannot truly exist between an individual and a fantasy, so every mystical event depends on our willingness to commit ourselves, sometimes in free-fall style, to something or someone outside ourselves. The mystery lies at the intersection of stimulus and response. Death is no exception. Death is by no means separate from life. We work on our deaths every day, choosing and molding their manner and even their time. We remark often on how a person's dying matches his or her life, on how it seems all of a piece with the way they lived. Or we observe that men and women face suffering and death the same way they weather life. We all interact with death every day, tasting it as we might a wine, feeling its keen edge even in trifling losses and disappointments, holding it by the hand, as a dancer might a partner, in every separation. We pump the soul into every mystery from within, from inside our own experience.

Some people are bitterly disillusioned by the realization that marriage does not take care of itself, that it is not a final goal but an awesome beginning. The mystery at the core of marriage is friendship; split its deepest seed and the mystery looms even larger: It catches fire only as persons respond to each other and it flourishes as they meet freshly in the midst of continuing change. Friendship is fine work at close range, high-wire work over open spaces, a great wholeness fashioned out of the smallest pieces of life every day. The mystical reality at the heart of friendship is more homely than exotic. Its face is that of everyday existence, of simple things whose power comes from people who can look at and share them together. But that takes time and effort and not settling for what one accomplished yesterday.

Friendship is sweet, but it is not all sweetness. The richness of its flavor derives from the strength of its ingredients, two real persons in contact with the truth about each other. The work of friendship lies in the steady effort to keep somebody else in clear focus, to keep listening even after you think you have heard everything, to understand when you would prefer to be understood, to choose the relationship knowing that it is not free, that there is a price to pay, a death to be accepted as the condition of richer life.

The human challenge of friendship causes us to pull farther out of ourselves, to reach toward someone else even though we must give up some protection and comfort to do so. A glimpse of the mystery is granted only to those who do lift themselves up and away from the comfort of a fixed position. Friendship is as wondrous as the dazzling world outside the mouth of the cave; it may be safer to remain inside, but those who surrender security find that their effort is rewarded by the subsequent discovery of the deepest of human experiences.

This exchange does not ordinarily take place in a self-conscious manner. We pull away from comfort without thinking about it because we want to make or maintain contact with another person. Just as we leave the nest of the cave in a natural move toward the warmth of the sun, so we move toward others without excessively dramatizing the effort that we must make in order to do so. It is entirely natural and healthy for us. Energy is expended; sacrifice is indeed made; there is always some cost involved. The activity on the inside of friendship is constant and its rewards of true union with another replenish our human stores. We do not count the prices of love, but that does not mean that we do not pay them.

Perhaps we only notice them, feel the heaviness of the challenge, when we are tired, discouraged, or when we have been hurt. Then we know that love and friendship do not care for themselves. We find that we cannot depend on friendship because, in fact, friendship depends on us. It exacts an extra mile, an additional investment of belief, a willingness to give when our bank of human gifts seems empty. The demand comes when we feel the tackiness of our own souls, when the world has been too much with us, when we feel like saying the hell with it. That is always the moment—and it comes often for most human beings—when we draw on our reserves. We also rise above ourselves and, without thinking explicitly about it, enlarge our souls. The mystery of life's meaning is delivered a little more fully to us every time we give of ourselves for the sake of someone else.

The activity of friendship is, for most people, the stuff of life. It is the center from which radiate those experiences and relationships that are the familial and social framework from which meaning flows. What makes friendship and love extraordinary is the human energy with which we power them. They demand what is best about our humanity. Whenever we are engaged—usually unselfconsciously—in responding to the normal demands of our relationships, we strengthen our hold on ourselves and our lives. We are closer to an understanding of both, not on some intellectual level through which we can spin a satisfactory theory to account for the patterns and the anomalies of existence, but like the music of a great composer or the pictures of a great artist, the work of friendship speaks to us at a different level, at the deepest level of our personalities. It symbolizes the things for which we have not yet found the words; it moves and changes us whether we are aware of it or not. That is why unlettered people can possess such wisdom about life, why they have a feel for its joys and its sorrows, why they understand what the learned often do not. They have been caught up in the expanding rhythms of birth, death, and resurrection. The work of friendship is our most humanizing experience. It draws us closer to ourselves, to another person, and to a better relationship with all persons. It makes us keener in our appreciation of the other mysteries of life. Only those who do the work of friendship can glimpse the meaning of sexuality, of birth and death, and of the ironic justice that life finally metes out to each one of us. They see, through the shadows of its brokenness, the wholeness of life.

What are some of these basic tasks of friendship? These are familiar to us already. They are high-sounding, they are rich in the things of the spirit, but they are not beyond any of us. Sometimes we know them better because we fail at doing them as well as we would like. These are activities that we pursue, that we get better at, but that we may never master completely. They are, in short, ideals; but they fit human nature. We are also tested constantly in trying to achieve them; we never can rest on our laurels and think that we have finally gotten them down pat. Every day is a new contest when it comes to having faith in and hoping for others.

Believing in others is a prime example of the work of friendship. It may be easy to believe in an abstraction, but it is difficult to believe steadily in a flesh-and-blood fellow human being. Of its nature, belief requires a

constant gift of our exposed selves. The word *believe,*
from the Latin *cordo,* means simply "I give my heart."
When we believe in someone else, we are not asked to
give intellectual assent to their being. We give a fully
human, entirely personal gift of ourselves. It is one of
those situations in which going halfway is the same as
not going at all. Belief, the giving of the heart to another, requires a commitment to another individual.
To commit means to entrust oneself to another. Everything, therefore, may be lost or betrayed at any moment. Belief is a dangerous business precisely because
it takes place between faulted human beings. Otherwise belief would mean nothing; it would have no
strength. There would be neither risk nor power in
this gift of the heart were there a guarantee that
things would work out, that nothing would go wrong,
or that, if it does, we could somehow get our hearts or
our money back.

There would be no need for belief if such guaran-
tees could be given, or if someone could sue successfully after the rupture of belief and get back their existential investment, plus punitive damages as well.
Believing lies at the foundation of the good life. To believe is a commitment of our whole being to the cause
of another. We cannot make such a gift of ourselves in
a void; we do it in the midst of the contradictions and
confusions of our everyday existence and to a person
who may abuse our gift. It is the very act of making
such a commitment, however, that integrates us, that
seals our identity more surely, that gives us a sense of
what life is all about. The biblical saying "your faith
has made you whole" describes it perfectly.

Believing in other people is, however, extremely
hazardous. That is why the good effects are so great
both for the believer and the one believed in. Parents

believe in their children and transmit to them the capacity to believe in themselves and others. They give them the strength to keep the race going with the only energy that ever really works. We cannot give that gift of our hearts without at the same time enlarging our own spirits. There are no points for grudging gifts, no points for pretense or manipulation. We either believe truly or we do not believe at all. Belief is, therefore, a heightened moment in which we rise above ourselves and transmit the essence of life to someone else. It is the marvelous achievement of ordinary persons that, despite their failings, they can still do this. Our own hearts are the source of mystical energy, our friendships are its celebration.

Being faithful, therefore, is a lively activity. We work at it all the time in the network of our friendships. Fidelity is not remembering a musty pledge from another time when we were different and did not know so much. Being faithful suggests that we continue to respond with the gift of our hearts to someone else, and that we learn to fashion that gift differently—perhaps more subtly, perhaps more urgently—as life works its changes in us and our friends. Fidelity does not require that we never change, but that we change constantly in order to be able to invest each other with the gift of our growing selves. A parent believes very differently but no less truly in a child who is fifteen from the way he or she does in a child who is five. Parents believe in grown children, although in a way that is enormously transformed from the way they believed in them as infants. Yet the ultimate nature of the belief—the gift of the heart—remains the same. Friends grow older, grow to be different in numberless ways, and yet, if they carry out the work of friendship, they steadily deepen their relationship. Bored people may never understand what is involved in giving themselves in belief to others or to the extraordinary world around them. Boredom is the death of belief in the possible, a paralysis of the spirit that strikes those who no longer make the gift of their hearts to others.

Belief in our relationships with others is similar to our responses to conditions and events, to the best chances that life presents to us all the time. A spring day may be gorgeous, but not if we refuse to give our hearts to it and stay in the house watching television. Gardening or good exercise is expanding for both mind and body, but not if we merely think about them. As we give ourselves to such activities we interact with the social and natural environment. Giving something, we receive something in return. We hardly ever lose anything by giving ourselves to the play and work that by their very nature match the genuine needs of human beings. We can be diminished—actually lose the edge of our existential being—by watching life from a distance. Television is no cure for human boredom; it is a symptom of the terrible disease that infects people who no longer believe in the possibilities of real life.

Through friendship we keep faith with our own best possibilities as well as those of others. That is why people who find new friends, or who fall in love, experience an increase in their energy level. The world suddenly looks different; what was commonplace yesterday is filled with magic today. Friendship, when we perceive it as something that we must work on rather than wait to receive, changes us for the better. It is a much healthier exercise than jogging, breathing deeply, meditating, or any of the other isolating self-improvement techniques of the age. Friendship makes it possible to share our play, exercise, or sorrow with somebody else; that is the key to the lock of life's meaning.

This is not to say that life is one great enforced recess period during which we must wear identification badges and get to know each other. Obviously, there is an essential place for solitude, for being alone, for respecting our separateness. These experiences cannot, however, be appreciated without the strong anchor of deeply human relationships. It is because we experience genuine—as contrasted to cheap and easy—intimacy that we can draw apart and reflect on our lives, or that we can give ourselves creatively to the necessarily solitary work of art. People who commit themselves to each other achieve the depth of character as well as the spiritual energy to carry out their other activities. Friendship is the base on which individual creative achievement rests.

As in everything connected with friendship, there are two sides to the issue of belief and trust. To give of our hearts is draining. To receive the heart of another is no less demanding. It is challenging to trust and challenging to be trusted. This, as has been observed, is work that can only be carried out at close quarters. The possibilities of something going wrong and of someone's being hurt are, therefore, very real. There may be no more humanly damaging experience than to believe and be betrayed. The real sacrilegious act of life is that through which we break fidelity, abuse the trust of another, destroy the bond that belief builds. It could not be otherwise. The human emotions involved in friendship are fissionable materials. They cannot be trifled with; one cannot shape a human or moral life on the notion that matters of intimacy can be indifferent. The exchange between friends is always delicate and there are always consequences for both parties.

Friendship is the best setting in which to witness the otherwise invisible mysteries that inspirit and transform our lives. How we behave with each other, whether we tell the truth or not, whether we are trustworthy or not—all these are at stake, all these are tested in close relationships. We cannot just *have* friends; we must *be* friends in return. Otherwise friendship is an illusion, a psychological distortion not based on reality at all.

There are, of course, pseudofriendships. These are relationships that arise from emotional problems rather than from psychic reality. Neurotic needs, for example, may draw people into relationships with each other that are based on what is unhealthy in their personalities. In a classic pairing, for example, an obsessive-compulsive person may be drawn into a relationship with an hysteric. The obsessive-compulsive gives order to the chaotic life of the hysteric, while the latter adds dash and vivaciousness to the staid world of the former. Is this a relationship that in its own crazy way works? Yes, and we may not wish to disturb it unnecessarily. Let people do the best they can. We would not, however, call such pairings friendship in the sense in which it has been discussed here. So too, some persons, occasionally those in positions of trust, form relationships with others that are gratifying to their own needs but that may be harmful to others. The boy-scout leader or the professor who seduces those who trust him can hardly be described as having given the gift of his heart to others. Such persons, masters of manipulating the trusting natures of others, take but do not give. They may, in fact, damage the persons whose trust they violate so that as a result they themselves have subsequent difficulty in trusting other relationships.

We can ordinarily identify these relationships in which emotional distortion predominates by observing their inappropriate character. There will be too much attention, too many favors, too much effort to guarantee that the befriended will remain indebted to the one who befriends. In real friendship, these elements—the give and take, the relative strength of one versus the other—are in better proportion. Pseudofriendships lack the human grace that is the hallmark of genuine friendship.

Talk of high ideals, of trust and truthfulness, of the need for health rather than emotional distortion—these reflections may cause us to shy away from the propositions of friendship. The tower seems so high, the nobility too lofty for the average person to aspire to success in such endeavors of the heart. There is something to the hesitation that one experiences at contemplating the majesty of transforming friendship. If it is an aspect of the grander mysteries, locked mystically even with death, how can the ordinary person hope to approach and not fail at friendship?

Genuine friendship, lofty and transforming though it is, still fits us very well. It is, above and beyond all else, a human experience. The best thing about real friendship is that it is not destroyed by occasional failures, it is not wrecked by our mistakes. Friendship is, after all, a relationship built across the jagged-edged space between human beings. An acknowledgment of the shortcomings of our human condition is built into it. Friendship is stronger than our weakness; it is, finally, what enables us, our faults thick upon us, to make it through life together. It can stand mistakes; it can survive the inevitable misunderstandings and hurts that are part of every human endeavor. Friendship knows all about these; its basic nature is to understand and to heal, to make room for the other who has had just as bad a day as we have. Friends are always leaning on each other, now my turn and now yours; they do not want to make things worse, but better. And that takes a great deal of compassion, steadiness, and a willingness to listen to each other's troubles. The main business of friendship is to sustain and make bearable each other's burdens. We may do more of that as friends than we do anything else. Getting through the tough times, offering encouragement when the other desperately needs it, shoring each other up to face the unfairness of existence—the main work of friendship consists of just such homely tasks.

Friendship, we might say, works when it is applied humanly. It never works, for example, if we expect a friend to be superhuman, if we hold out expectations that no other person can ever meet. In friendship there is a large margin for error, and there is a great necessity for patience. Because friends see each other clearly they know each other's basic strengths. They also know each other's weaknesses. Friendship allows us to keep these in some manageable relationship to each other. All we need, after all, is to be a little stronger than we are weak and we will get along quite well in life. Friends make this possible for each other.

The truth, then, is that the virtues at the heart of this great mystery—believing and trusting—are never found in a pure and unalloyed state. We may have to look closely to find them at the bottom of classically human situations. Great belief, for example, may be transmitted between friends when one is listening somewhat uncritically to another as he or she complains about something. On the surface, this is a scene we see many times each day. What transforms it is the patience and understanding of the listening friend.

The powerful mystery is cloaked in the commonplace appearance of the exchange. Yet beneath that ordinary transaction we witness friendship in the authentic human range. The fine nerve of belief snakes through the grunts and silences; the woman believes in the man complaining about the hurt he has sustained at work. She gives him back his belief in himself, not through some grand gesture or dramatic statement, but in the steady, utterly human manner in which the riches of the spirit are transferred from one individual to another. She listens, she makes room again for the injured man, she gives him time to complain, to explode the bombs of his anger, to voice hints of discouragement. Friendship works in just such settings, in the unspectacular events that constitute the happenings and meaning that hold our lives together.

Perhaps the main work of friendship is to nourish and sustain the myth of each other's personalities. We believe in each other's strength and by doing so we actually increase it. We stand by and endorse each other's ambitions and thereby make them more attainable. We encourage each other to reach our ideals. Trust and truthfulness, shared in the slightly shaded way of everything human, do get across and have their enlarging and transforming effect. These indispensable sources of our human development are transmitted even in the quiet moments of friendship. Just knowing that our friends are there, that there are those who believe in us, motivates us powerfully when we are away from them. Friendship finds distance and time no real obstacle. The wonders of tomorrow's communication devices, existing perhaps only in the imaginations of science-fiction writers, have been known to friends down through the centuries. The marvel of it is that our most mystical experiences are bound up in our most ordinary moments. Friendship is stronger than time and is not intimidated by distance. It does not wait for the grand entrance or the dramatic event; it permeates the lives of the truly human. It is the quiet witness to its own wonder, stronger than death precisely because it is so filled with the ultimate strength of life itself.

What do friends reveal to each other? They may take off their clothes, but that, of course, does not necessarily reveal anything about their true selves. Nudity may, in fact, obscure one person's vision of another. It corrupts the vision entirely if it is motivated only by an interest in surfaces. Our culture has suffered from an obsession with surfaces. Beauty has been defined as skin deep to the impoverishment of our concept of beauty and to the bitter frustration of those who do not know how to get beneath appearances. Narcissism is a block to friendship. Those who suffer from it cannot reveal much of their inner personalities because they are hollow, dug-out creatures, mocking their own best possibilities by their shallowness. Such persons are destined to have unrelieved problems in their relationships. Although they may know how to expose themselves, they do not understand how to reveal themselves. They need our compassionate understanding far more than any condemnation because, exiled from the Eden of friendship, they are sentenced to live with their own images alone.

NINE

Friendship as an
Unreasonable Activity

In the long run, life is not rational at all. It is poetic. And the poetic bear it away.

That is just another way of saying that life is human and that nothing that is human is ever quite as simple as it seems. Men and women do not function reasonably, but that does not mean they lack purpose or direction, only that they function humanly. A dried-out actuary calculating cost-benefit ratios would probably conclude that friendship is not an efficient enterprise. Entirely too much time is wasted, and the outcomes are difficult to measure. There is too much of that "down" time so dreaded by people who love the thrumming of computers. You cannot make sense out of friendship, the accountant would complain, you cannot put it on a business basis.

We can all live with the conclusion that friendship is not a business venture. We have no wish that it should be. We cannot, however, accept the closely related conclusion that friendship and love cannot be logical.

We would like it if there were rules that held for various situations in our human relationships, rules to which we could turn, as players turn to a referee, to settle disputed points in matters of the heart. Reason, however, cannot be applied cleanly and coolly in issues centering on friendship. When one spouse says to another across the battlefield of the breakfast table, "Let's be reasonable about this," we can be sure that is exactly what they will not be. It is not in the human way of things, not at all, and those interested in understanding friendship must learn this truth in a practical way. We live in and through many layers of personality and, although reason may be the topmost, it is not everything and it may not even be the most important.

Perhaps it would be better to speak of the logic of personal living, which is quite different from syllogistic logic. It suggests that there is a pattern to the way in which we live with each other, one more like stock-market tables—that is, heavy in psychological components—than an astronomer's table of eclipses, which is heavy in mathematics. Our existences have a shape. and we can develop a feeling for that shape, for the way we bulge out here or the manner in which we pull back there. If we listen we can overhear ourselves talking with some appreciation for the inner determinants of our moves and choices. "I always do that." "I could have told myself that I'd do that." "I wish I had listened to myself." Such remarks are evidence of the existence of this mysteriously moving subself, this commenting, criticizing aspect of ourselves, this person who seems to be within us, catching cues and giving off signals, monitoring impulses and making connections for us.

It is crazy, we say at one level, for us to think about

ourselves in such a manner. We are, after all, logical, reasonable human beings. And yet, at another level we recognize the distorted but observable logic of our comings and goings. We get to know something of our feelings and of our unconscious life; we understand that sometimes we receive clear messages on those levels that we could never put into words. They defy logic and yet they are full of information. We react to other people, for example, on this inner emotional level. We can, in fact, trust our psychological reactions about other people more than the reassuring judgments of our intellects. "I had a feeling there was something wrong there. He just didn't make me feel right. I wish I had paid attention to myself." This may not be reasonable, but there is an indisputable logic to the soundings that come from deep within ourselves. We give ourselves good counsel. We are friendly to ourselves when we give ourselves a chance.

As we sensitize ourselves to those inner realities— as we, in other words, respect the complexity of our personalities more—we become aware of elaborate psychological relay stations in other persons. Indeed, with friends, our reactions are often on the deepest levels of personality. The chemistry, as people call it, of relationships is actually one way to describe the many ways in which messages are exchanged between people. When we understand the unconscious, we comprehend its protean logic and can understand our human way of communicating much better.

Putting aside for the moment the amount of static that may clog these channels of communication, especially between people with psychological problems, it is obvious that friends become highly attuned to each other's emotional rhythms; they learn to "read" each other with amazing, wordless accuracy. This ability to sense the distorted logic of each other's personalities, this capacity to hear and understand the slightest variations in mood and tone—they enhance friends' responses to each other. Friends who read this poetic language of the total personality know when and how to reach out to each other. Friends who are sensitized to each other's inner stirrings also know when to leave each other alone, when not to press an argument too hard, when to let an interval of time and space shape itself naturally between them. This only sounds complicated. Friends do this for each other all the time.

Once we understand the richness of our personality construction, we live with a different sense of time and place. Once we appreciate that we are not summed up in this surface that is now showing, in this timebound, distracted, overly logical entity we call the self, once we know that there is more to us than what we think about so reasonably, we become more comfortable with ourselves. We live on friendlier terms with ourselves. We are aware of the timeless aspect of our unconscious selves. We may feel the tide that cannot be measured, the tide that passes and yet never moves, of our individual life history. We will not be surprised at how much of what we have seen and known impinges on the illusory present moment of our lives. There is more to us than we suspected and the kingdom of God is indeed within us. It is that kingdom that we throw open to another in the mystery of friendship.

We have many languages for speaking to this complete self, to this subject of inheritance and experience, to this altogether remarkable person, full of surprises, who is really us. And we use these languages to speak to the full selves of others. We speak symbolically as well as logically; sometimes we whisper and at other times we convey and receive messages intui-

tively. When we are generous and loving, we give
something of all of this richness of personality to
others. We do not know how much of ourselves we
give; we cannot count or identify all the elements. Nor
can we measure everything that we receive in return
from the stores of another person. That is why friends
are presences to each other and why they cannot ex-
haust each other's wealth of human character and
qualities. So rich are we when we make available the
true fullness of ourselves, that there is always more to
give and always room in which to receive from the
other.

Again, there are hints about this in the way people
who love truly speak about each other. "There's a side
to him that only I can see." "You'll never know how
gentle she is." "I wish others could know the man that
I know." "If you knew Suzie . . ." All are reflections in
the same glittering pool of human mystery. This is,
however, very close to the bone of friendship. Real
friends hold open house in their psyches for each
other; they can wander about, picking up now this and
now that, familiarizing themselves with the territory
like unsighted persons sensitively establishing a map
of a room. Friends pick up the messages from the
deeper structures of personality; they sense them even
when they cannot find the right words with which to
describe them. They respect each other's inner territory, as a great friend respects another's home, but
they are comfortable in it. Knowing they are welcome,
they understand that their presence makes a difference—often crucial—to the other. Friends pump life
into each other. When we speak of the intimacy in
which this happens we speak of no easy thing. We
refer, rather, to the way in which friends gradually
make passages across each other's borders, of how

they come to rest easy in a world that is much more spacious than that of their own egos. "Deep speaks to deep," we read, and "heart speaks to heart." We have known about this for a long time.

Cronies and acquaintances may know many things about each other, but they do not communicate in and through the levels of personality that are engaged in the mystery of true friendship. Male bonding leads to good times and great adventures, but it does not necessarily generate the kind of friendship that is at once illogical and profoundly meaningful. One of the most touching evidences of this truth emerged from a study of clergymen made some years ago. Through in-depth interviews they spoke reflectively about their lives. A great many of them described their clerical associates—their golfing and drinking companions, their "friends"—and then confessed that, despite the camaraderie, nobody really knew them well.

The word *friend* should be reserved for those relationships that literally go beneath the surface. Real friends do exactly that even when they do not understand fully how they are involved in the deepest layers of each other's being. They commingle without running together in a glob of protoplasm from which their own identity can no longer be extracted. The mystery of friendship—the genuinely mystical aspect of it—consists in the everyday miracle by which two individuals, without losing themselves, are able to give the gift of their hearts to each other. The heart has always symbolized the inner self, the multitiered display of our uniqueness, and it is exactly what we freely pledge in the belief in the other that is so central to friendship. Cooks speak of "marrying" flavors; they unconsciously use the symbolism of marriage to describe the interpenetration of essences that is the object of their art. It is a refreshing use of a familiar word for it describes this totally illogical but finely textured way in which people draw close and blend with each other in the friendship of marriage.

The word *friend* has been debased by its easy application to lesser relationships. We have not thought long or hard enough about the wonders of friendship marked by this communication between persons. It is not just habit or familiarity that makes close friends feel incomplete when they are apart. It isn't merely that they are "used to" each other. They are saying that, when they are separate, something is missing. It is a death, another signal of the constant intermingling of these mysteries, a loss of the fuller sense of themselves that people experience in genuine intimacy.

The extraordinary capacity of friends to send and receive messages to each other on so many wavelengths surprises only those who have never broken out of themselves enough to take the soundings of another human being. Sexuality is, of course, one of the languages that best carries the message between people who love each other. Many persons, dazed veterans of the sexual revolution, are returning to the idea that sex only takes on meaning in relationships that are more than casual. Nobody, of course, is ever going to eliminate the impersonal sex that is in itself more a signal of desperate loneliness than a celebration of Eros unbound. People, are, after all, only human. They seek, finally, those experiences that make them feel more rather than less human. There will always be those who remain at the subhuman level of their social and sexual functioning. Their capacity to choose more ennobling relationships is compromised by conflicts that are too much for them. Exotic and kinky sex we will always have with us, but these are signs of something wrong, not something right. If we could look deeply enough into the impulses beneath what we term "perversions," we might even discover a human signal, a stunted and crippled longing for friendship, a sad flickering testimony to frustrated human growth. That is not, however, our main concern. We want to place sexuality in the context of human relationships that are in the range attainable by most relatively healthy people.

Sexuality bears the weight of multiple communications from the varied layers of our personalities. It enables us to speak to each other and to share richly the contents of our personalities even when we are not completely sure of what we want to (or urgently must) tell each other. Sexuality is the great vehicle for the communication of everything that is in us; it says what we cannot otherwise say. We must, however, learn to speak the language of sexuality—as friends, not competitors, not enemies—to each other. We get better at the language of sexuality only if we take the time and effort to do so. Like everything else connected with friendship, it does not take care of itself. Sexuality is a language designed to be spoken by two people. It fails if it is used only to express the demand that one person makes on another. It is a language that is meant, in the tide of pleasure that sweeps through the transaction, to empty and fill us with each other. Sexual union is the perfect symbolism of persons who are attuned to each other's depths. Sexuality is a peaceful and profound communication—wholly illogical, of course, and not explained well in charts, graphs, and orgasm counts. Sexuality is intensely personal. It becomes boring only for persons who see it as an end in itself. It never bores those who keep each other in view; they want to tell each other something rather than prove something. They have something to share, not something with which to test each other.

For most people sexuality is an extremely important part of life. It takes on a settled quality when it is understood as the way people say everything they want to each other. There is more to them than the notions that crowd their heads and the distractions of the day, and sexuality provides a simultaneous translation, at a level below conscious awareness, of our deepest longings and most significant truths. It is no accident that friends speak of keeping "in touch" or "making contact." These are small, familiar hints about our great need for physical closeness, the indispensable instrument of healthy human relationships. One of contemporary society's great problems lies in its desperate efforts to understand everything about sexuality. It is not meant to be understood fully. It serves us well when we don't have it figured out. We are friendly to ourselves when we allow it to retain some mystery.

Friends get to understand these truths through encountering them together. They come to recognize them after they have suffered disappointment and frustration, for example, by trying to use sex as a way of friendship. It works the other way around. Friendship is the foundation for a satisfying sexual life. Its experience with another human being is an adventure in exploring the depths of each other's identities. Sexuality is not something we will ever understand fully. How splendidly human! Seen in the context of the human scale of friendship, sex is comprehensible and natural, just like friendship itself. It may not be very logical, but it is meaningful, full of wonder, a magnificent seal on our humanity.

TEN

The Ages of Friendship

FRIENDSHIP and love grow only because we work at them. That process always includes some element of dying. The mysteries of friendship and death grow together like graceful vines curving up from the same plot of earth. Touch one and you touch the other. Friends maintain their friendships, not through Rotarian heartiness, but through a spiritual commitment to the value of what they are together. That is what they are willing to die for. A relationship thrives only if two persons both value it more than themselves, more than just getting their own way. Friendships survive, quite simply, because people want them to; they can also die, usually at the hands of one or both of the persons in the relationship. There is no expanding life for a friendship unless the persons involved are ready to surrender something of themselves—to die at least a little—for each other's sake every day.

This ascesis of friendship is the basic reality that writers on the subject often choose to ignore. They sometimes tell people how to get around the hard truths of human relationships, or how to get their own way in them, but they hold back from pronouncing a truth that is as ancient as any that we know: Loving depends on giving, happiness is stabilized by sacrifice, life is given to those who are willing to die. The question of whether a relationship develops and survives the changes wrought by time and contingency can be answered only conditionally. If friends are willing to let go of themselves, they never lose each other. If friends are ready to surrender the position they reached together yesterday, they will pass successfully toward one they will achieve tomorrow. The rhythm of friendship is as natural as any found in the universe. Friendship lives in and through adaptability. That is the law for all living things.

A man and woman who are still in love after twenty-five years of marriage have died to and for each other in a thousand small ways—neither can claim a lasting victory for this to work—throughout their pilgrimage. They have taken the deep breath and made the effort to face difficult truths, to work through disagreements, and to travel a long road of understanding to find each other after something has broken their stride together. It is a dynamic condition, always shifting, always demanding something new, filled with unexpected and, at times, unpleasant surprises.

Friendship does not sound like fun when these somber notes of sacrifice and inevitable change are sounded. Yet these are necessary experiences for anybody who prizes joy more than pleasure. Friends come to share a kind of happiness that cannot be taken away from them. It rises off their relationship, created by just such a human joining, the sparks of contentment leaping unmistakably between the persons as an electric charge does between two terminals. This contentment, marked by peace and certainty, is a byproduct of the commitment that friends make to each other and to their relationship. It cannot and does not enjoy a separate existence; its spirit is born in the reciprocity of lovers' responses to each other. It is what comes, as naturally as sweetness from a rose, from the combination of human effort and understanding—and a certain familiarity with death—that builds a friendship in the first place. Marvelously enough, this byproduct, this abiding sureness in each other's presence, cannot be lost, stolen, or ravaged by time. It is what survives after accident and change to strengthen persons for the next lap of their journey together. As long as they can reach toward each other, it is present; as long as it is present, they will continue to reach toward each other.

Time and circumstances test relationships. Some, like poor roofing in a windstorm, lift away and are quickly scattered. Such relationships were never truly secure, however, nor made of the enduring qualities that are necessary for lasting friendships. A storm arises and it is gone even if it looked somewhat like a friendship to begin with. The truth and falsity of friendships are gradually revealed by the tensions that build up on the arc of time. Sooner or later every relationship feels the stress of disagreement. People look at each other in a slightly different fashion and decide that they have never seen each other truthfully before that moment. Others become aware of the imbalance that always existed in the relationship. It may take a long time for this to happen—such things can be very subtle—but, sooner or later, the fault in the structure of the relationship will be tested and revealed.

It may, for example, take some time for a person or persons to realize that they are being manipulated by someone who, on the surface, seems a good and loyal friend. But this individual exercises extraordinary control in his or her relationships. That may not be noticed until an individual dissents or decides to do something in a way that the controlling pseudofriend dislikes. It is precisely at this point that the manipulators of relationships exhibit their true colors. They withhold approval; they use a combination of guilt and shame in order to bring others back into line. This is a familiar dynamic in human relationships. Almost everyone has been in a relationship with these characteristics at one time or another. They readily and perhaps ruefully understand the pressure that builds up in such circumstances. They know that it is not easy to escape the situation. The controller, master of the psychological carrot and stick, knows how to dangle favors and gifts in front of rebelling "friends." Such behavior, often evinced in people who otherwise seem benign, is first-class evidence that no friendship ever really existed. Persons caught in such uncomfortable binds need to break free—no compromise is really possible with such power manipulators—no matter what the cost may seem. It will be cheap in the long run because such relationships are dead ends; they are used chiefly for the disproportionate gratification of one person and friendship can never work on that basis. Such relationships should be pronounced dead and given a dignified funeral with no exhumations allowed at a later date.

Some friendships are temporary. They seem to possess a half-life, as though their whole purpose was to offer support at some important interval in our lives and not to live beyond that. That is understandable in shipboard friends or in other relationships that are limited by a set of temporary circumstances. Still, for the time they serve both parties well, and we should not weep unnecessarily for relationships that worked for part of our journey. Such friendships may come into our lives, for example, during periods of transition or adjustment. They are just what we need at the time and they strengthen us and prepare us for the next move we must make. They are whole and entire experiences and we open our handclasp and release each other when they are done. That is one of the ways in which we encounter the mystery of death in the experience of friendship. We must respect all the messages we receive from others and from ourselves. Otherwise we would fail to respect ourselves and the meaning of the relationship, howsoever brief, which we shared with someone else. A person may be an extraordinarily helpful friend for the length of a plane flight and then pass out of our lives for good. A kind of death, yes, but with a heritage of life trailing after it.

Friendship, like all living things, has a natural life cycle. We cannot expect it to be otherwise. The best approach to friendship is one that appreciates its naturalness, its fittingness for human beings. Friendship does best when it is not celebrated melodramatically or sentimentally. Nature does not *overdo* things. And neither should we. The more we press for, manipulate, or otherwise try to control friendship, the more surely will we stunt its growth or destroy it altogether. When we understand friendship as a natural occurrence, we are not surprised that it may grow in different forms, or at varying rates, and that some may live longer and give greater pleasure than others. We can never be surprised at the relationship of death to growth, or at its ultimate necessity in the passing seasons of our relationships.

Friendship is what we all look for, even when we do

not recognize or admit it; it is a prize that matches the
needs and aspirations of human beings. It fits us and
allows us to know who we are and more besides, for it
is a mystery filled with hints about the meaning that
rises up from our everyday longing and heartbreak and
laughter.

As eager as adolescents to taste its bittersweet wonder, we sometimes define friendship falsely, idealize it
excessively, or, with no perspective on the way our
own needs conspire unreasonably against our best interests, interpret it solely in terms of what it can deliver to us. Nothing may be sadder, and nothing more
certain of disappointment, than the quest to "find" or
to "win" a friend as if friendship were a commodity of
which we could be consumers. It is more natural than
that.

Friends are discovered the way we find a charming
route home, without road maps or plans and with only
our openness to guide us. We fall over friends the way
heroes in mythology stumble and discover gold, and
like them we sometimes do not understand our good
fortune. Friendship grows naturally if we make room
for it and respect its inner truth, but it withers (as a
healthy plant does) when we interfere too much with
its innate pattern of development.

Despite the blunders so often associated with our
search for friendship, nothing is more poignant or
more truly reflective of what human beings are like
than the core of the friendship experience. People are
not really looking for much; they seek someone else toward whom, in a profound way, they can reach in continuing commitments of faith and hope and love.

Friendship energizes all of us to a sense of life. How
could we ever enter the river of existence except in the
company of someone else? What else could friendship

be but finding a person with whom we can stand comfortably on the edge of mystery and pain, with whom we can discover wonder and joy, with whom we can weep or laugh or do nothing at all? Friends are not just people with whom we share activities. They are people who, quite literally, let each other be.

There is a sweet naturalness in understanding friendship as something that matches us so well and that can be found without heavy breathing or excessive dramaturgy. There are surprises and anomalies connected with this understanding of friendship. It is possible, for example, for people to be friends even though they do not know it. They are ready, nonetheless, to recognize and respond to each other when they finally do meet. They have been mysteriously prepared for it. They feel that they have known each other for a long time. They may, in some sense, be right. Because they possess the same natural sympathies, they have already shared a common view of many people and events. They have sighed or been filled with wonder at the very same sights, all unknown to each other. But what they have already shared is there within each of them when they meet. Is it possible that such people are drawn invisibly toward each other, meeting against all odds in the strangest ways? We have all seen such things happen. We cannot make them happen, no matter how archly we may plan to do so. These things do occur, we say, acknowledging a natural truth about the cosmos and the nature of the friendship that seeds it.

If we are wise we watch and learn friendship's lessons just as we do all things that are natural. If we overromanticize friendship we treat it poorly; we fail to respect it on its own terms. Such distortion means that we may not recognize true friendship when it does occur precisely because we are expecting something fancier, gaudier, or more intense. We will be able to live through the ages of friendship and to sense its constancy in the midst of change.

Friendship, like the world around us, demands that we observe and understand it, that we try to interact with it on its own terms rather than attempt to subdue it. Understanding, that patient effort to see to the bottom of things, to catch the current, to sense messages bubbling up, now singly and now in clusters, from the deepest parts of ourselves, is indispensable to an appreciation of friendship as a profoundly natural and human experience. We will then strain less for it and be far more receptive to it when it comes, as it does so regularly, into our lives.

ELEVEN

Separation—
Common Denominator

FRIENDSHIP prepares us for death because it enables
us to meet, live with, and conquer it throughout our
lives. Separation is the common denominator of both
death and our living human relationships, the inevitable component at the heart of each. Wherever and
however we turn, we confront these interlocked mysteries. To deal with them we look directly at the experience from which, as though by ancient instinct, we in-
voluntarily pull away. Gaze deeply into the crystal eye
of separation and see the split reflections of friendship
and death. Separation is, in fact, the one thing we can
be sure of in life.

Like a microscopic view of a razor blade, the edge of
existence is scored with the imperfections that symbol-
ize the way separations are integrated into life. The
more fully alive men and women are, the more keenly
they feel the deaths of every day, the pulling apart that
is more familiar to us than the big losses or the small
partings that are sometimes anything but sweet sor-

row. There is no friendship without a sense of the dying that goes into it.

We are up against our limitations all the time, angry at the seeming death to relationships and love that they press on us. Periods of time, even when they are relatively very long, hardly seem that way in retrospect. A long time, when it is used up, as it is for the widow by the coffin of her husband, is not so long at all; it is not nearly enough time. Is childhood ever long enough, or a happy time, or even a beautiful summer day? All of these carry the seeds of the same fierce mystery that we call death. In many ways we work all through life on a problem that finds its own symbol and solution in death itself. That is the problem of separation, a reality that is as regular as the tides in every life. Separation is the seam that joins friendship and death.

The modern world deals with death in the fashion it does—through so much denial or manipulation—because it is so frustrated and bewildered by the many-sided experience of separation. Separation is a riddle and a test, something we would never feel unless we were truly alive, but something into which we find ourselves falling as though captured by the pull of death itself. Separation spreads like a shadow across life and yet, denied light by it, we can still see to the far goals of wisdom, creativity, and happiness. Separation is like a blade that cuts across our strongest impulses to unite, and to be one in love. In some way that passes understanding, separation seems essential if love is to achieve strength and fullness. Nothing pains us more than separation, and yet nothing confronts and challenges us more as we pursue the tasks of friendship that are the basic challenges of life.

Birth comes as a separation from the floating and

secure world of the womb. Life proceeds, as Otto Rank once explained, through a series of separations, and the outcome of each is crucial for our personal development. The cup of separation is filled with bitterness, but we must drink it because of an inexorable law: Either we learn to separate ourselves from our past or we will be separated, by fate or other forces, anyway. There is no question about whether we must, for example, separate from infancy and childhood. The only question centers on how we do it. A species of death, then, stalks our healthiest growth, just as it does for every other form of life. We have to shed the past and surrender our toys and our magical view of the universe; we must allow innocence to die in order to achieve a scarred but durable maturity. Is there a place in all these passages and relationships on which the shadow of separation does not fall?

We die and rise, sure as the seasons, and we are never done with it. Just as we get our breath back from surviving the minor deaths of one difficulty in living, we find that, with hardly a pause for a rest, we are challenged once again. We must stare into the darkness just at the moment we thought we had gained the light; we must begin planting again just as we thought we were ready to enjoy the harvest.

Separation is at the heart of the major tests of growing away from adolescence or separating ourselves from our previous history by recognizing the humanness of our parents or the faults of our country. There are also infinitely small experiences, registered on the eye and heart in a fraction of a second, filled with all the power of life and death. These are the moments in which we glimpse the beauty of the world that we cannot close our hands on, the beauty of a loved one we suddenly see afresh; so we see our own selves, as we

are surprised by our unretouched features in the reflection of a store window, and know that, even though
we feel young, we are growing old; and sometimes the
melancholy burden of existence strikes us as we see
the dead in the light of day. Author Loudon Wain-
wright, writing of the cross section of present and past
he sees on the streets of New York, described this well:

> And the dead, of course, are walking around town,
> too, caught in glimpses down the block—a certain
> thickness of the neck, a longish stride in the rain,
> the way black hair falls on the shoulder. I've
> learned not to try to overtake them.
> ("Faces Passed," *New York Times Magazine*, Dec.
>   18, 1977, p. 48)

Something truly dies in us as we feel the small rents
in our hearts that go with the sweet remembrance of
what seem to have been sunlit spaces in our lives,
those periods filled with hope and expectation because
we could willingly give of ourselves in anticipation of
the successes and rewards that lay ahead. And yet
there is death and separation even in success because
its achievement means that life has already changed
and that, if some of the striving has ended, so too has
some of the special happiness that always accompanies
it. There is a kind of death, a real separation for parents in seeing children grow up, a dying to themselves
that is an extension of the love of their mothers and fa-
thers who understand that separation is an urgent aspect of their lives.

If we count the separations in any average day we
begin to appreciate the unfolding nature of this reality.
The cosmic drama of separation may be found in the
mystery of light and darkness; the human drama is
reenacted in every simple leave-taking and homecom-

ing. We also sense how intimately the acceptance and actual suffering of separation are linked, almost as breath to life, to a deeper penetration of existence, to a sense of how separation, a fissure of death across the world, is at the same time a bridge to a deeper and broader life. We yield ourselves up and, instead of permanently losing ourselves, we find ourselves again. We look into death's face a thousand times before we die; we have seen it before, a likeness as close as that of the dead who do walk the streets, in every separation that we have lived through actively. And there is a measurable difference between that and the passive endurance of separation. We triumph over death in some degree; we find it less strange, when we are able to separate ourselves from people and events rather than merely being separated from them.

This is no invitation to masochism. God knows there is enough human energy wasted in the neurotic expiation of guilt—and this is yet another mode for our experience of separation in the splits that emerge between our ideals and our behavior—but separation, in its most finely honed state, is found all the time in the lives of relatively healthy persons. "Relatively healthy" is the only phrase to use in describing the best of us; imperfection is itself a signal of normalcy, and separation is one of its stepchildren. The world we inherit is flawed and we can live in it successfully—and begin to understand its meaning—only when we look directly at it with the sharpest eyes and accept its mysteries and its capacity to hurt us.

Separation is a terrible reality for the modern world because it challenges the widespread unrealistic ideals of instant gratification and easy intimacy. Ordinary people have a sense in their bones, however, that they cannot have everything all at once, and they are ready to make sacrifices to achieve lasting values. The road to maturity begins in this mystery of separation that is at once filled with the mystery of death and the promise of life.

Psychoanalytic studies have underscored the importance of the process of separation as the infant moves gradually away from total reliance on the mothering figure. This initial exploration of the world is a hazardous adventure and separation from security is its essential condition. For persons to become individuals they must move away from their past, no matter how stable or wonderful it was. They must also be allowed to separate from it in order to achieve an independent life. This scene, so crucial in personal development, reflects the compelling drama of ongoing life and the endless separation that must be entered into with intermingled pain and joy, and in order to move to new levels of maturity.

Separation is a dappled mystery at best and it may be understandable that some people do everything they can to avoid it. But avoiding it, as in the case of the parent who will not let the child separate, only causes greater misery and death later on. There is something fundamental to understand here, something intimately connected with the meaning of death and friendship and our attitudes toward them.

Two realities confront us. Life is steeped in deaths of various kinds. When we try to ignore them or somehow distort them, we not only fail in these attempts, but we also make life, in the long run, more painful for ourselves. We harvest what we try to eradicate. On the other hand, when we can accept separation and death, we find that we actually open ourselves to greater life. We gain something because, in facing the gap of separation, we also find the way to bridge it successfully.

This understanding is essential to breaking out of narcissism and to finding friendship and conquering death.

The gap—at childbirth, adolescence, in various phases of adulthood and old age—is ever present. It may be *the* fact of life, the cleft at the bottom of so many other problems of ours. Trying to deal with its presence in our affairs—for even in the midst of our most intimate relationships it can assert itself—is a central task and a basic condition of living. Our human development is keyed to our capacity to separate ourselves from others through individuation so that we can draw close to others in adult relationships. We must be allowed to be separate before we can join ourselves to another.

Separation may be masked in other events, but its power can be identified if we look closely enough. It is at the core of one's first explorations outside the family; it throbs in the experience of friends who move away; it is the central aspect to loss, whether of persons or objects, at every stage of life. We are forever dealing with separation and loss, forever caught up in making passage across the spaces that open regularly in our lives. There is a foreshadowing of death in friendship and in every worthwhile experience of life.

It is surprising to some to discover that even in the midst of a great love this exhausting challenge presents itself. There is a "little death," as we have noted, even in sexual relationships, a mystifying reluctance in the heart of things to allow union without a certain amount of distance. Lovers need some separation in order to see each other better and to keep each other in perspective throughout a lifetime. They need the asceticism of this special dying if they are going to enjoy life together. Separation puzzles the ardent and makes friends patient in their capacity to endure the fissures of distance that break under their feet all the time.

Death is present in these events as it is in the various partings and surrenders that come with the middle and late years. Death foretold somehow in each of these experiences, death linked always with friendship, confronts us with the raw force of separation. There is something intractable about it; but there is also something familiar about it. People who have faced separation squarely in their lives are not overwhelmed when they have to let go—or let someone else go—in the mystery of dying.

It may be that Americans are intensely preoccupied with death as a final act because they have not paid enough attention to its appearance in so many other places in life. They neglect, indeed they misread, the nature of separation, perceiving it as an evil to be avoided or overcome. They are, therefore, less prepared for and more puzzled by death than those who have become acquainted with its power in all the many incidents of which it is a part. Death cannot be approached as an experience that can be separated from life. It is, rather, a culmination or a full flowering of an existence in which it leaves its mark and symbol at every turn.

Death is as intimately related to life as spirit is to flesh; it is like a sheath on the tissues of every nerve and vessel, the finest of linings in the robust and busy organs of heart and brain, a field force generated by each lively step or bold aspiration, the mystery we must face and live with in order to be friends. We carry our death with us, if not as a final groan of surrender to the seemingly unknown, then at least as a faint but discernible tracing in every human experience. This is not the death that, according to the saying, the coward must undergo a thousand times. It is the pain in the willingness to let go that is the necessary condition for our embracing anything or anyone; it is in the readiness to sacrifice that accompanies anything that is truly valuable; it is the losing of one's life in order to find it. It is the soul of friendship.

Forms of death also face us in all the reminders we have of the shortcomings of our human situation. It resides in injustice, cruelty, pettiness, and every failure to live up to our possibilities. A form of death lives its strange half-life in what we call sin, in the gulfs we create between ourselves and our ideals as well as between ourselves and others. And death lives all too powerfully in the events in which no one seems to blame, in tragedies and accidents, all of them scored by the acid of separation, or in the breakup of families or marriages in ways that no one would wish and yet ways that many cannot avoid. Separation is all around us, displaying images of death, involving us, whether we like it or not, in its programs and unforgiving mystery. Could we get through any of these if we did not also know friendship?

Death cannot be put off; it is the other side of every day's experience. We prepare for death, not by a morbid preoccupation with it as a single event, but through encountering it in the course of a life intensely lived, that is, one in which we face the nature of ourselves and our world as honestly as we can every day. We deal with death when we are strong enough to be friends. There are no tricks involved in this highly serious, although not oversolemn, approach to existence. It does imply that we best prepare for death, not by planning what we will do *then* (e.g., go to a hospice, take easing drugs, reform our lives), but what we do *now* (e.g., enter into the myriad separations that are essential to rich human relationships). Friendship bids us to embrace separation, giving rather than just taking, living for others rather than for ourselves.

There are no tricks that work on a mystery as grand and inviting as life anyway. The failure to see and work through the tasks of separation with which we are confronted even into old age may be one of the reasons that people have been so fascinated by death, so frightened by it, and like embalmers, so willing to retouch it cosmetically. Death, however, cannot be altered by powder or paint, or by a thousand plans to manage it and the grief it produces more efficiently. Death hurts, but so does life as it instructs us in the rudiments of the mystery of friendship. Looking into hurt and separation, facing and bridging the gaps by the powers of our spirit, we live by friendship because in it we learn to master death. Death, for friends, asks no more than they have already learned, many times over, to give.

TWELVE

Simple Things:
The Sources of Meaning

WHAT can be seen better if we look at it in the company of a friend? Love gives us the courage to inspect just about anything. Standing with others strengthens us to go through the worst that life can hurl at us. It also allows us to enjoy fully the best of its surprises and treasures. A spring day is improved when we walk through it with someone we love. Indeed, Elisabeth Kübler-Ross reports that dying patients remember just such events. Simple things flourish in their memories, while more elaborate experiences of wealth and fashion fade away to insignificance. Dying people recall good times—the family gatherings, the times with others that, viewed from death's perspective, were filled with life.

The precious moments may not be recognized as we go through them. They are the times in which we are called out of ourselves. We remember their warmth later on, sensing their depth, recognizing them as *the* good times during which we tasted life freely because

we tasted it in the company of others. We face here
another paradox connected with friendship and death.
The events brimming over with life are those that demand a death from us. What could that possibly mean
in the context of our considerations?

Friendship and love are successful in proportion to
our willingness to break the boundaries of our own
self-absorption. We achieve the vitality of free relationships with others only as we die to our own selves to
make room for others in our lives. The secret that is no
secret about friendship resides in self-forgetfulness, in
living for others rather than just ourselves. Persons
preoccupied with being number one can never relax;
they are constantly anxious and on guard lest they fall
to the number-two position. Men and women who put
the concerns of others ahead of their own are free of
such worry. They are free in the most essential and
fundamental manner, free of the weight of their own
ponderous egos.

We can enjoy the simple things of life when we respond unselfconsciously, when we die, in a real sense,
to the bloated and ravenous ego, when we lay down
our lives for our friends. Death as the condition for
life—it is a law from which none can escape. The poor
person who truly loves possesses far more of the universe than the greedy person who sees others only as
potential predators. Afraid to lose anything, the latter
cannot hold onto anything comfortably. Unafraid to
lose everything, the lover enters life confidently. We
see more of life when we look at it with others. We see
more and we share more because we make room for
the presence of other people close to ourselves. The
secret is in making that space available, in taking
others in, in seeing them as they are and appreciating
their viewpoints. We do that by ceding some of our

own rights. The effect, of course, is not to feel depleted by what we surrender, but to be filled by what others share with us. They literally restore us. Remarkable! A truth as old as any we know. Let it come any closer and we would fall over it. Most people know this already. They need to be reminded of it and of how much they gain title to in life through making willing sacrifices for love.

Why do people have to come close to dying in order to sort out the real blessings of their lives? Probably because they have not had the time to look back, probably because in busy and crowded lives we cannot really forget ourselves and worry about whether we are having a good time or not. The mother responds to her children for their sake. Out of love she surrenders sleep and accepts inconvenience. Her focus on her children's needs is so clear that she does not count or even observe her own sacrifice. The dying person has no choice about what is remembered. He or she still does not recall the deaths, the sacrifices that had to be made. The best memories float effortlessly to the surface of consciousness, revealing themselves as the treasured moments of the well-lived life. They constitute the inventory of a person's blessedness, the sweet images, cleansed of terror, that are the signals of happiness.

These are simple things, all of them, purchased at the price of self-forgetfulness, the self given up and found again. The close relationship between letting go of ourselves and our discovery of our true selves—between death and friendship—is not a somber prospect. Once the premise is accepted, individuals discover that life—even one that goes unnoticed by the media—is memorable indeed.

To the *right stuff* of courage we may add the *right*

things of life experience. These are the experiences
we go through together, the ones we could never comprehend fully alone, the events that deliver life fully to
us. We are, if we are the least bit separated from total
self-concern, caught up in the defining experiences of
existence. We may not call them that because their
face seems so ordinary. Yet it is in these that we are
called out of ourselves and through them that we pass
quietly through the doors of mystery. Transcendence
wears an everyday face.

We have made a great deal of separation in its various forms, in its mystically ascetic hold on our lives. It
is indeed a profound mystery, and we are caught up in
it all the time. In one of his short stories, John Cheever
writes of a man waiting for a train in the Indianapolis
railroad station. He is struck by the old structure's re-
semblance to a cathedral. There are great distances,
stained-glass windows, and the benches resemble
church pews. Then the appropriateness of the situation—its sacramental parity—strikes him. In railroad
stations we celebrate the mystery of travel and separation. It is no accident that the old station, harboring a
century of partings and reunions, should have a religious shape, that its atmosphere should be heavy with
the weight of life.

Separation is the inner seam of our comings and
goings. How much of life is centered on coming together and pulling apart! Anything meaningful includes some element of separation. We cannot escape
from it; we would not know ourselves without it.
Friendship and love, which depend on union, would
have no strength or weight if they did not incorporate
separation into their essence. There is a key here that
all must grasp to open the great door of life.

Return for a moment to the railroad station, to that

site we inhabit temporarily, often at moments of extraordinary human significance. People leave home, separate themselves from their families for the first time, in railroad stations. Men leave for war or for a new life. The train bears those who move and those who mourn. The railroad station is the scene for separation of every kind; it is the background, in other words, for those experiences of life that sum us up, that define us, that allow us to see the shape and substance of our lives. We are always on the move, coming and going, drawing together and pulling apart.

There is another side to the ubiquitous mystery of separation. That is return, homecoming, the reunion of loved ones, the countless comings together whose meaning is heightened because of the separation that has been endured. Can we name a great love in fact or fiction that has not been well acquainted with the small and large deaths of separation? Love that lasts needs the test of separation. It will surely undergo it. Fidelity expresses its meaning as much when people are apart as when they are together. Being apart is a necessary condition for any relationship. A puzzling aspect of the great mystery of friendship is that even those who love each other deeply often must draw apart. A husband and wife share the hospitality of their home with friends and discover at the end of the evening that they have spoken to everyone but each other. There is always something tugging at the bonds of friendship—duty, emergencies, illness, the numberless exigencies of contemporary life.

We are all caught up in the drama of heroes, all called upon to reenact in our own lives the mysteries that are profoundly human and mystical at the same time. The *right things* in our lives resonate with the challenges faced by gods, heroes, and saints throughout history. Thus the husband or wife leaving home in the morning relives the hero's departure from his native land to do battle with the world. The return in the evening, even when obscured by the blur of family activity, is that of Everyman caught up in the essential mysteries of life. The return is the seal on everything humanly prized, the completion of a cycle known well by every man and woman who has ever loved or taken the world seriously. We are acting out the great mysteries all the time, enduring separation, tasting something of death, finding each other again.

A dozen other examples of how we must let go of each other in order to be able to embrace each other later come quickly to mind. We cannot escape the interplay of death and life. Relationships of friendship and love define us humanly and we never lose them as long as we do not clutch them too tightly. We kill them when we fearfully hold onto them. We possess them forever when we accept the daily deaths that are the price of giving others true life. We are, in fact, engaged in activities of which separation and reunion are significant dynamics every day. These are what we remember and still possess even as the shadow of death falls on us.

We speak, then, of no small mystery but of the heart of the mysteries of friendship and death. We die to ourselves as we make true friends. This experience fills us with the life that is stronger than death. Bound together, interwoven, and unyielding to gimmicks, friendship and death are the symmetrical mysteries into which life inducts us all. The experience of separation is inescapable and difficult to postpone without doing psychological damage to ourselves and others. The boy still "tied to his mother's apron strings" is but one character in our folklore about the inevitability and the necessity of undergoing separation.

Parallels may be found everywhere. Artists undergo a kind of separation—a dis-integration, a death to their present adjustment—as a necessary condition of reintegrating, of making a fresh vision of life whole in their creative work. Creative friendship demands the same in a life that will not stand still. We are forever readjusting ourselves in order to keep in dynamic balance with those we love. Give up the dying that goes into the constructive regrouping of the self and we surrender to the sterility and aridity of an isolated and unnourished existence.

Separation and other common experiences possess what can be termed a sacramental significance. Sacraments and rites of passage always focus on significant junctions in our lives. They underscore them for us with a ritual that deepens our understanding of our human development and our relationships with each other. Thus confirmation in its many religious and cultural forms celebrates an important point of change in our lives. So too do the rites of initiation, marriage, and community membership. They serve to raise our consciousness and, through the symbolism and the ritual, to enable us to look deeply into our lives, to see, even briefly, into the heart of the mysteries of our existence.

Separation is a common feature of many of these sacramental occasions. The most powerful religious rituals, such as the Eucharist, are actions commemorating separation, drawing our attention to it, symbolically allowing us to incorporate its broader meaning into our lives. Our separations, small and great, may then possess a profound religious and mystical significance. The whole idea of religious and other rituals is to enable us to see the seemingly simple events of our lives in a larger historical and theological perspective. Religious rites do not possess the mystery. They point to the mysteries with which we are in daily contact.

Even a partial review of these deepens our hold on life, on our identities, and on those elements of our everyday existence that are authentically mystical. We stand in the sacramental old railroad station in many different ways. As we recognize these—and most center on friendship and love—we gain a much better and more reliable understanding of our lives. These are simple things, almost all of them, but portals of transcendence too. We do not make mystical passages by way of drugs or chants. We make them every day in the small but extremely significant ways in which we embrace friendship and confront death.

Take beginnings and endings. Life is crammed with them. They are immensely significant to all of us or we would not remember birthdays, anniversaries, or occasions of memorial. Each day has a beginning that re-creates on a small scale the start of our lives and our pilgrimage. We enter consciousness again and pull ourselves together for the struggle that will either enlarge or diminish us. Beginnings are always there, even when we think we have finally passed well beyond them. How common the feeling, even into old age, of needing to start again, to adjust to new circumstances, to prove, after we thought all the proving was done, that we can handle the challenges of life.

"I am the Alpha and the Omega," we read in the Book of Revelation, "the Beginning and the End." Why should we be surprised to find our lives seeded with beginnings, with the need to start freshly? There is a new season for the star athlete, a new play for the

great actress, a blank page or an untouched canvas for
the creative artist. They are never "done" any more
than life is ever "done." Beginning again is central to
being human. "Having it made" is an illusion, an ulti-
mately stultifying state for men and women. Beginning again may seem vexing to them, but it is essential
to their survival and their flourishing as human
beings.

Friends begin again all the time. They may be able
to count on a store of understanding and shared experiences, but today will be different from yesterday. The
tests are slightly changed and yesterday's answers no
longer work as well as the ones that must be fashioned
freshly today. Friends do change, the years do inter-
vene, and unless they keep up with each other, they
may find that, if their friendship is to survive, they will
have to begin all over again to get to know each other.
Is friendship still friendship for people who only meet
at reunions and tell the same war or college stories all
over again? They may do it heartily and with genuine
enjoyment, but they frequently have a bittersweet
awareness of the gap of experiences that now sepa-
rates them.

Remembered friendship is a real entity, but even at
its best, it is not as vital as the living friendship we
need to work on every day in the present. Husbands
and wives are always beginning again with each other.
Their relationship will not become dull if they realize
how filled their days are with the need to begin again.
They begin afresh, for example, when they can forgive
each other and forget what they have done to each
other through misunderstanding, forgetfulness, or
general human weakness. The ability to begin again is
the first practical act of faith that friends make for

each other. Believing in someone else means, on the realistic level, giving them a fresh slate, a new beginning with every day.

People speak of the beginning of a new life, as they do, for example, on their wedding day. They talk of a fresh start, a new job, a different house in a different city. Beginnings each of them; sacramental all of them. Perhaps we should speak of happy beginnings instead of happy endings. Beginnings bear the weight of our faith in each other. They are all possibility; they are, as people often say even after great achievements, the best times of their lives. Beginnings, at any stage, are not to be neglected. They are the daily business of human beings, the essential work of friends.

Beginnings, of course, make sense only if we speak also of endings. These are the natural correlates of all our beginnings. We speak of the end of childhood, the end of innocence, the end of a happy period in our lives. We stand together at many endings and friends must understand these as sensitively as they do the mystery of beginnings. The year ends and another begins, a job ends and another task crooks a beckoning finger at us. These phenomena are always linked. Endings and beginnings are the deaths and resurrections of our lives. We must attend to them, acknowledge their significance and impact, and not ignore or try to make an end run around them.

Endings confront us again with the losses that fill our lives, with the sense of death as the fire in the eye of life, of death living with us, punctuating our days, touching our lives somehow in every hour, if only in the sound of the time that ticks away. Endings prepare us for death itself, for the end of what seems familiar and proper, for the opening of that last door and our passage through it. Only those who know the discipline of the many endings within life can confidently face the ending of earthly life itself. They know how to die because they have seen separation and death at work, as much a part of life as anything else. They have met them before. Death is no stranger to them.

The endings in life must be faced as realistically as possible. Things do end and we must have a feeling for this if we are not to deceive ourselves. Even friendships can end, even marriages can be pronounced dead, even the liveliest of our human associations can come to the end of their natural cycle. We cannot hold onto the most beautiful of days, and sometimes we need to let go of relationships that are just as beautiful but can no longer be sustained. There are limits, for example, to our expectations of friendships that can no longer be supported because of intractable misunderstandings. We sometimes must let them die. We may mourn them and we may feel regrets, but the mystery, confounded and unfair, will work its way with us. We may become estranged for a variety of circumstances from once seemingly close friends. Perhaps the occasion of the estrangement permits us to see that the relationship was not as deep as we had supposed. The ending of it may allow us to see the weaknesses that we did not allow ourselves to perceive earlier. We may at last observe ourselves and our own motivations clearly from the termination point of a friendship. This is not to make of this a good thing. It is, however, realistic. It is also testimony to the quirky nature of mystery, to the unanticipated ways in which we face loss and separation during every day. We live in mystery; we see flashes of it in every beginning and ending. They haunt us as first words and last words do; they are significant and must be felt; even though they are painful, they are signals that we are alive.

Beginnings and endings are found scattered throughout the context of our relationships. Because we have friends we are able to deal with their two-sided challenge. One way or the other, these starts and finishes, these taking things up and laying them down, constitute a large part of our lives. They are functions of the grand mysteries of friendship and death and they will always be with us.

An even more delicate fiber of our lives together can be observed in something we often dislike and almost always try to avoid. Waiting is the ingredient, part life, part death, halfway between beginning and ending— waiting, the strange, omnipresent interlude between what seem to be more important events. But is the waiting so aimless and meaningless, is it just the entr'acte of our homely existences? Or is it powerful and meaningful in its own right?

How much time do men and women spend in waiting? Look at the filled waiting rooms in doctors' offices and airports. Are we always between journeys? Have we always just finished one and not quite begun another? "You'll have to wait; your tests didn't come back from the lab"—or your suit from the cleaner, or your pictures from the developer. Or it is late and your spouse has not yet returned from work or an appointment. What has happened? What might happen? Fear can mount quickly as we wonder in moments of waiting about the fate of our loved ones. We do it constantly, and the agonizing moments allow us to see what we feel about each other. We get a good look at ourselves when we observe ourselves waiting.

Waiting is a part of small and great experiences. What happens in the months of waiting for a child to be born? This is waiting filled with life and change, waiting lifted to the level of expectation. Yet it is waiting, and it cannot be hurried; to have its full effect it must be endured. Delay, that contemporary enemy of digests, crash courses, and instant gratification, may be vitally important for human beings. How else could they understand and absorb the meaning of their richest experiences? These need time to sift down, to settle within us, and to become part of us. We need intervals to grow and to heal and there is no substitute for these periods of waiting, no way to do away with them. They are profoundly significant and essential to our humanity.

Friends must understand waiting. There is no friendship without it. We are, after all, never quite on the same schedule; waiting for each other to catch up in one way or another is a commonplace in good relationships. There is more than a hint of death in waiting. We come up against restraint and the frustration of our impulses in periods of waiting. We learn in our patience, according to the Bible, how to possess our souls. So friends may pass through a period of waiting, of tentative exploration, before they yield the gift of good relationships to each other. Friends learn each other's idiosyncrasies and personal rhythms. They wait, as spouses do, for the right moment to say something, or to propose something. Knowing how to wait is indispensable to friendship. It is also part of the larger, miraculous mystery in which we lead our lives.

Friends die often to their own wishes as they live out this unexpected mystery of waiting. Sometimes they must wait for themselves, knowing that they are not wise enough or strong enough to carry out some proposed task. And sometimes, in great pain, friends must wait for each other when they don't want to wait at all. Friends, after all, do hurt each other. That is the hazard at the heart of the mystery. They may wish to seek forgiveness and to patch things up. There are instances, however, when the wound still throbs too much, when the injured one cannot yet be approached. The hurt is too fresh and the friend who wishes to apologize must wait—there is a true death in this—before forgiveness can be sought and reconciliation can begin. Part of loving others depends on being able to wait for them. Just as the seasons are marked with waiting, in the same way that the Churches declare times of expectation in Advent before Christmas and Lent before Easter, so the rolling mystery of existence is also marked with waiting. Nothing is more natural or more common. What are we waiting for? the old question goes. Usually, for each other.

These are only some of the dimensions of the mysteries of friendship and death with which we live all the time. Mysterial experiences always surprise us with their familiar faces. We have seen them often. The small miracles that attend our relationships with each other are the only ones we will ever need. It has been observed that the real reason people go on pilgrimages is so that they can return home with a clearer vision of what was there all the time. Our pilgrimage has returned us home, to our daily lives, to the wonders of what, as friends, we go through together all the time. But everybody knows that already.

THIRTEEN

Hard Questions about the Mystery

Our mistake has been to imagine that mystical experiences take us out of life. They do just the opposite: The truly mystical phenomena bring us more deeply into life. They allow us to see what is really there, to make sense out of the collage of our seemingly routine days. Mystical experiences constitute a revelation. They shake the pan of silt lifted from the river of the ordinary so that we can see the flecks of gold that have been there all along. Mystery rises like a cloud off the surface of every day, bidding us to search within life for its origin. The real mystics see into things, people, and events; they see down to the core with an intensity that casts light all about it. They give us the illumination we need to understand the mood of revelation that hangs over our human comings and goings.

That light enables us to understand friendship and death as related mysteries. We glimpse their detailed engagement with each other, their intimate infiltration of each other in our own lives. We sense the transcendent features of these intertwined mysteries as we follow the course of every authentic relationship of love. They are present any place people make a difference to one another.

If the experience of friendship opens us to the spiritual character of our everyday exchanges, it also acquaints us with the rough practicalities of life. A mystical experience makes everything more clear, the sheer and glorious highlands and the rough and broken slopes. If we have a better feeling for the transcendent wonders of our lives, we also have a better understanding of the utterly realistic issues connected with friendship. True mystics are not dreamers. Real friends cannot be dreamers. They know the difference between fad and fancy, kinky and healthy, what friends are and are not to each other. Mystical experience leaves clear heads behind.

On the practical level, then, individuals who are truly friends keenly understand the nature of friendship. They are not shaken or put off by fads or fears. They know, for example, that friendship is buffeted by opinions that come and go, that it can often be a victim of shallow fads and trendiness. It is strong enough to survive such onslaughts quite well. Despite the clarity of this truth, friendship has had some difficult cultural moments lately.

Although friendship—that luminous and enlarging move out of the self and toward another—seems to be recognized by everybody as one of the first great mysteries of growing, and despite the banners that reassure us that friends divide our troubles and double our joys, despite Kahlil Gibran and the longings of all the world's lonely people, something has indeed happened to the market value of friendship. Why have these troubles arisen about friendship? Three contemporary attitudes are worth inspecting: Friendship is *impossible, too dangerous,* or *just possibly grounds for indictment as homosexuality.*

Some believe that friendship is impossible because no relationship of any lasting consequence can ever be achieved. To support this viewpoint they cite our complicated psychological mentality, noting that the best of persons spend a lot of time sorting out the false from the true aspects of their personalities. People often build bridges from a phantom and unreal self that they do not acknowledge or understand to an equally vague surface image of another. They do not really meet; they just get entangled in each other's webs. Only after long periods of thinking that they know each other do these supposed friends discover that they do not even know themselves very well. What they thought was present was more illusion than reality. Novels and movies are filled with such groping men and women, people who seem to fall into friendship or love and grow bitterly out of it, convinced by the cold stone of alienation weighing down their hearts that people can never really share, that life, in some poignant and final sentence, condemns us to walk its long corridors alone. This is the painful conclusion of many: Friendship is a snare for the naive and the overoptimistic, something we would all like but something none of us is ever destined to possess.

Friendship is also ruled out of bounds as too dangerous for us. The danger springs, oddly enough, not from the illusion, but from the reality of friendship. People may become friends all right; they may even come to love one another. But inevitably, they will kill each other off with the hurts they exchange once they live at close range. That is why so many friendships fall apart; the risk is just too great, and if you let people see you as you really are, they are bound to take a shot at you while your guard is down. Even lovers do it, the scarred and weary will tell you, and it is small wonder that so many friends, even in marriage, drift just far enough out of each other's range to prevent any damage from the gunfire that goes along with intimacy. What they do, consciously or not, is adjust to each other rather than work steadily at being genuinely close to each other. Many people make a truce with life and their chances for love—by not expecting too much, by learning how to minimize conflict, and by living a kind of affable coexistence that, if it is not deep and reaffirming friendship, is at least free of the wounds this dangerous commodity visits on those who take it seriously.

If this were not trouble enough for friendship, our culture—the arts, letters, and cinema—has been telling us for some time now of the growing suspicion that homosexuality runs like a river through even the best same-sex friendships. A recently revived notion says that there is no friendship like that between a man and another man; that, after all the paeans to the man-woman relationship have been sung, the boys must still band together to become fully masculine. All this good fellowship in bars and duckblinds is to some avail after all; men finally redeem each other, backslapping and bullshooting in the all-male atmosphere of ultimate masculine invigoration. But, perched like an expectant vulture on a limb high above all this, a close-eyed bird clucks that such brotherhood is bonded by homosexual motivations; that men, of all things, are secretly meant and long for each other. Well, this has given men a little pause about their bonhomie and introduced a note of suspicious caution into their feelings about friendship.

There is another aspect to this issue of homosexuality, of course, one that capitalizes equally on the American tremors about being queer. This can be seen in the use of homosexual accusations in the running battle between certain women's lib leaders and their male chauvinist counterparts. Why else, the indicters ask, should these men and women be so defensive about their gender? The charge of homosexuality has, in other words, become an assaultive weapon in a psychologically minded age; it is better to be on guard against it than, through too much spontaneous friendship, to lay oneself open to the charge. What about these charges?

Impossible? In many ways, friendship is the least likely thing to find in an inconstant world; and yet it is a part of a larger understanding of love that, in fact, heals the wounds of the embattled universe and makes life possible. Friendship would have little significance if it were an easy goal or a simple and effortless achievement. The wonder of friendship is that it is God's gift to a broken world, a truly "amazing grace" that defies the laws of likelihood and challenges the charges that it is impossible. People who believe friendship is impossible because of man's psychological complexity forget that friendship is tailored expressly for the psychologically complex person; friendship fits men and women as they are rather than as they might ideally be. In other words, friendship is not reserved for persons who, after years of analysis, are keenly aware of every one of their psychic kinks and deceptive motivations. Being friends would be an icy business in a landscape of personalities forever freed from the emotional earthquakes and flash floods of the human condition. Friendship is available, not just to the perfect, but to every person who is willing to work at it and not be afraid of spills and hurts now and then.

Friendship, however, is impossible for those who, perhaps to avoid some of its potential painfulness, try to make it happen instantly or without effort. There is a large measure of delusion in the promise—made by a variety of groups, from those who practice sensitivity to those who pray together—that friendship can grow out of a mere few hours or days together. Cervantes wrote long ago that "a man must eat a peck of salt with his friend before he knows him," and that still holds true today. The kind of friendship that is truly impossible is that which people try to accomplish by short-cuts, the painless *Reader's Digest* version of what is essentially a continuing story.

Dangerous? To this charge, of course, friendship must plead guilty, if dangerous is the correct word to describe the state of lowered defensiveness that must develop. Friendship is dangerous for the very reasons that life is dangerous: Take it seriously and something is liable to happen to you. Not all the possibilities of life or friendship are, however, sinister; the person who tries to avoid all dangers had better live in a museum than in the real world. Running risks, as we are forever reasserting intellectually, is essential for any kind of life; the trouble is that the risks are emotional—that's where you get hurt in the guts, not in the head. And hurt is the biggest danger in a phenomenon as sensitive as friendship. You just cannot have friends without this dangerous possibility any more than you can have an ocean without water. Eliminating or attempting to overcontrol the possibilities of danger just kills off the substance of friendship altogether. But friendship is also quite durable when it is real, and it offers strength and protection against the danger even as it makes us vulnerable to it.

Friendship is most dangerous to those who expect it to be so. Friends, after all, support each other much more than they hurt each other. But individuals who overplay their concern about the dangers of friendship reveal an uncertain outlook in themselves that almost surely makes friendship dangerous for them. The question that must be asked of these persons is this: What are you afraid of? This is a particularly good question when the individual who expresses concern is actually meddling in the lives of other persons. It takes more self-confidence than most of us possess to pass judgment on where, when, and how persons can be friends to each other. Good example is better than bad advice in this regard. As a matter of fact, the best thing that anyone who is preoccupied about the dangers of friendship could do is to emphasize the development of solid and mature friendship in his or her own life. People learn more about friendship and the way to handle its dangers successfully from observing the manner in which genuine friends get on with each other than they do from an armful of warnings. Friendship is dangerous in the way that all precious things are; it may be misused, misunderstood, or even lost. This does not change its value, however. It merely emphasizes the essential importance of our active commitment to friendship.

Homosexual? People who get too shaken up about the hidden homosexual implications in their relationships become very self-conscious and, if anything, more rather than less unsure about themselves. These homosexual accusations have been quite overdone; it is a sign of emotional immaturity to consider the charge of homosexuality a bludgeon to use against others anyway. And it is a sign of the fatal brand of romantic homosexuality to insist that all friendship that is noble must, in fact, be basically homosexual. Persons should not be surprised that homosexual feelings are part of life for everybody, but they should not be thereby appalled nor unnecessarily defensive as a result. Man is a complex reality and he takes a long time to grow; the easily generated specter of ever-present homosexuality can only make mature growth more difficult for the great middle range of healthy persons. It is obvious that shying away from friendship because of a fear of homosexuality only reflects a deeper set of personal uncertainties in those who take the threat seriously.

Some Myths about Friendship

The Friends-Tell-Each-Other-Off Myth

This myth is currently popular because of the distorted view one gets from looking at reality through the eyes of confrontation-therapy enthusiasts; it is their version of the ill-tempered cry about the source of political power, only now it states that "all relationship comes from the barrel of a gun." To be close is equated with the freedom to fire on friends at will, to tell them, in exquisitely detailed terms, everything that is wrong with them. They, of course, are supposed to remain your friend through this stormy weather; at least they are not allowed to flinch or they will be penalized for copping out on what is good for them. This myth generates a curious tension; it becomes a magnetic force pulling people toward it; once under its spell, they find it difficult to disengage themselves, as though they were irreversibly committed to hostile exchange as the only way of "opening up" to one another. A lot of grim-looking people seem to believe that this is the only mode through which friendship can be achieved and maintained; to them, free-flowing bile is somehow an anointing of the Spirit.

Upon close examination, friends who insist on the right to tell you off may not be friends at all; in fact, they may be quite lost in their own inner confusions, meeting needs that they have not learned to name by directing their anger outward. Friends who define their relationship to you solely in terms of their own feelings ("You make me feel uncomfortable when you talk about that") are clearly individuals who have not emerged from their own world of special self-concern. They aren't finished pecking away at the shell of their own narcissism; friends who talk about their own reactions all the time are not yet mature enough to give or to receive friendship coming from confrontation; it makes life a lot easier but not any more rewarding for them.

The Friends-Are-Always-Together Myth

This is a notion perpetuated by the emotionally needy, the persons so fearful of losing their friends that they never let them out of their sight. True friendship, however, is made to survive separation, even as, in the long run, it is meant to survive death itself. If you take a close look at the lives of people who are true friends to one another, you discover that constant closeness is not an absolute requirement for their relationship. As a matter of fact, one of the best measures of friendship is how well it flourishes when persons are, for whatever reason, separated from one another. There is a deep mystery in this, to be sure; it is strange that a relationship in which people long to be together is so often characterized by their being apart. This is true in the most profound relationships of love; as life progresses, as children come and obligations accumulate, even the most devoted husbands and wives find that their moments of being quietly and completely together become fewer and fewer. Their friendship—and anyone who does not realize that lovers must also be friends has a great deal to learn—must be made of sturdier stuff than togetherness. Friends who do not realize this—who are made restless and anxious about what their friend is doing out there somewhere without them—are really experiencing their own lack of maturity in the fact that they are not peaceful in the relationship. Friendship that is true is an almost indestructible commodity; it can stand the ravages of time and distance; it can take the minor and major separations that demand patience but build peace in the sharing that is the richest of our spiritual experiences.

The Friends-Always-Feel-Deeply-about-Things Myth

Closely related to the foregoing, this myth claims that every moment must be severely taxed of all the emotional content that it possesses; that friendship cannot be friendship without heavy breathing and soulful glances; that every meeting of friends requires a baring of the soul, a confession of the week's secret anguishes. Actually, friends are supposed to be able to enjoy each other in the very simple but deep meaning of that term: They must be able to be relaxed and at ease in each other's presence, able to be quiet or just to smile in common appreciation of some shared event. Friends are the people you have fun with, not the ones you must wrestle with in spiritual discomfort at every meeting. The friendship that generates tension, like a hum around high wires, is artificial and will quiver and snap under strain. Genuine friendship has a lot of give in it; it seldom needs to be drawn taut.

The Friends-Never-Let-You-Down Myth

This is the unrealistic kind of myth that leads us to make impossible demands on our friends—to expect them to be lesser gods or at least mind readers who always respond in exactly the right measure to our needs. As a matter of fact, in the human condition the best of friends are bound to disappoint each other at least once in a while. The marvel is that authentic friendship endures despite these cracks in its facade. Friends need not be perfect friends in order to be very good friends; lasting relationships, wherever they are found, bear the scars that go with the hazards of living.

Persons who demand a perfect friend or lover are merely condemning themselves and the relationship to a larger dose of frustration. The miracle of grace that supports genuine friendship resides in the way people who wound each other are capable of healing each other, in the way people who fail each other can also forgive each other. Friendship is not a smooth rink on which a marvelous and errorless brand of figure skating goes on without even scratching the surface. Friendship is a broken turf, full of the promise of spring, but also marred by the ditches and holes in which friends may stumble as they try to stick together. Friendship is an imperfect work if it is anything, something we get better at if we make the effort every day, but never glossy smooth at any stage in life.

The Friends-Have-to-Take-You-as-You-Are Myth

The operative word here is *have*, because if friends *have* to take you, then they are being friends on the terms you dictate, and that is the death of any genuine mutuality. Now it may well be that good friends do take us as we are, but they do so freely and without compulsion; their friendship is an act of love and not an act of duty. Many people, however, feel that there is no burden on them to modify themselves in order to make themselves more worthy of their good friends. It is, of course, very convenient to skip this self-examination and to place all the responsibility for patience and understanding on those around us. In reality, this myth is just an offshoot of the myth that makes our own reactions the complete measure of our willing-. ness to relate to others. The sad thing about individuals who believe that the burden for accepting them is on their friends is that sooner or later, when there is no equal pulling of the weight in the relationship, friends begin to drop away one by one. People who always want others to accept them end up alone with the great love of their lives, themselves, and may always wonder why. The answer is simple: They never got far enough out of themselves to be a friend to anyone else. And they were never really friends to themselves.

One final word must be said about friendship: You cannot buy it or wheedle it out of others successfully. The truest path to friendship lies in the effort to make our best selves available to others, to strip ourselves of the obscuring dross of selfishness, and to give more than we demand. The man or woman who becomes even partially mature—who displays a real rather than a false and ensnaring self—will discover that friend-ship happens in a wonderfully natural way and that it does not need to be manufactured.

FOURTEEN

The Right Place,
the Only Place

"EARTH'S the right place for love," Robert Frost
wrote. "I don't know anywhere it's likely to go better."
Earth, of course, is the *only* place for love and friendship, the only place for all of us working our way
through the only mysteries that really mean anything.
We are working on the meaning of our lives every day
that we work at being friends to each other. That is the
task, in the long run, the only one worth our human
sacrifice and energy.

Friendship is obviously a journey rather than a goal.
Perceived as a termination point, friendship is a trophy, a stuffed souvenir of a prey conquered long ago.
Friendship is not an artifact for our collection. It is a
living, breathing, and altogether central aspect of our
lives. We could not survive without it. We are only
human when we pursue it. That pursuit involves us in
something that many people want to abandon: the patient effort to understand, the untiring work of compassion.

It is easy to tire of being understanding. There are signs of people and movements pulling back from the spirit of understanding that, despite everything else, did flourish over the past twenty years. It is not just the governmental hardliners in international policy; it is also the tough, we've-had-enough-of-compassion thinking involved in reducing social programs and educational support. We can see it in the retreat of the Churches from their profound ecumenical overtures during the sixties and seventies. One can sense it in the culture's burnout with trying to deal with racism, poverty, and similar questions. The move toward insularity, toward complacency with the self, is well advanced. "The hell with it" may serve as the grim slogan of the eighties.

We can only respond effectively on the individual level. We do it by working at friendship even when we are worn out by the effort. We rekindle the mystery every time we make a real effort to reach out to each other. Friendship is as much a national need as energy.

So it is in our individual lives. We need each other more than ever just as we are sorely tempted to give up on each other. We need each other to get the strength to refurbish friendship as the renewing mystery for our time.

We may best begin that task and end this book with a recognition of the difficulties involved in all human relationships. Friendship, as has been noted repeatedly in these reflections, demands a commitment of our persons in a very demanding way. There are deaths every day in loving others—death to the selfish ego that wants to turn in on itself, death to the impulses whose unthinking gratification has been easily and cheaply rationalized over the last several years.

There is nothing easy about becoming a friend. It requires maturity, self-discipline, and a willingness to be understanding even when we are tired of the effort.

But there is nothing like friendship, nothing better for all those around us. The joy of friendship makes its sacrifices far less difficult than they would otherwise be. The sense of ourselves delivered by friendship is unparalleled. It is absolutely the right thing for us struggling human beings. It is with that overriding understanding that we turn, sometimes with anxiety and uncertainty, to every day's work of friendship, the affectionate miracle that plunges us into the midst of mystery and reveals the world to us.